Ladybank   Lochty

h Leven

Burntisland   Gullane

of Forth

Princes Street   Dunbar

Waverley   Monktonhall Jct.

DINBURGH   Monktonhall Jct.

Millerhill Yard   HADDINGTON

Grantshouse   N.B.R

Falahill Summit   BERWICK   Berwick

Fountainhall   Lauder

B‾LES

PEEBLES   Galashiels   N.E.R

SELKIRK

Jedburgh   Alnwick

SELKIRK   ROXBURGH   BORDER BDY

NORTHUMBERLAND   N.E.R

Riccarton Jct   Rothbury

Steele Road

Langholm   N.B.R   Morpeth

kerbie   Reedsmouth

C.R   N.E.R   NEWCASTLE

Gretna   Hexham

CARLISLE

M&C

LNWR   M.R   Alston

D1492403

Roaming the Scottish Rails

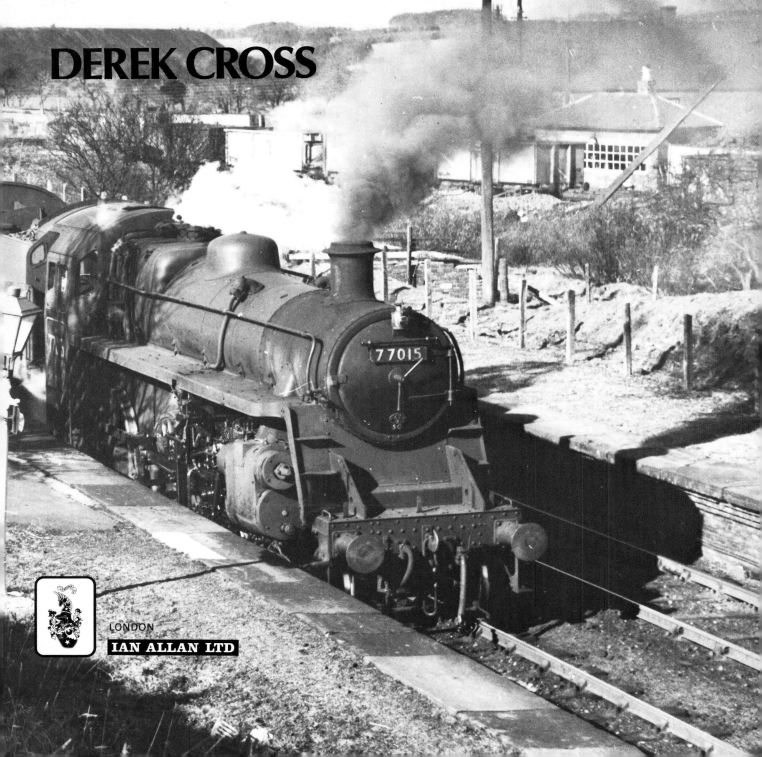

Roaming the Scottish Rails

DEREK CROSS

LONDON
IAN ALLAN LTD

'To my wife without whose constant opposition many of these photographs would never have been taken'.

First published 1978

ISBN 0 7110 0855 8

Published by Ian Allan Ltd, Shepperton, Surrey; and printed in the United Kingdom by Ian Allan Printing Ltd

Contents

Foreword   7
Preface   8
The Debatable Lands   11
The Caledonian Line from
    Gretna Junction—Glasgow   21
The Nith Valley Line and branches
    Glasgow/Annan   57
Edinburgh, the East Coast and
    Waverley Routes   91
The Central Lowlands and Fife   119
Stirling to Perth and the
    North East   139
The Highlands   153
Ayrshire and Galloway   175

Foreword

For many years Derek Cross was, to me, a name under a picture in one of the railway publications. Very good pictures they were (and are) too. I heard that he lived somewhere the other side of the Roman Wall — rather off my usual beat. I thought that sooner or later I should bump into him at one of the better-known haunts of railway enthusiasts. The actual day of meeting eventually came on 31 August 1975, which, as all railways enthusiasts know, was the date of the Steam Cavalcade at Shildon. It happened like this. The yards at Shildon were teeming with people, and the only hope of taking photographs with so many people about was to get above them. Two of us had the same idea. One was Derek Cross the other was me. We both spotted a staircase leading to a platform outside the Manager's Office. We arrived, blowing a bit, almost simultaneously at this excellent vantage point. Neither of us knew who the other was, but it was not long before we did. I introduced my Rolleiflex to Derek's Rollei 66, and then followed the usual sort of chat that you get when two photographers meet. This meeting added greatly to my enjoyment of the day. Soon we separated to hunt separately. The last time we met was in pouring rain at Carnforth when *Hardwick* was piloting *Flying Scotsman* to Hellifield. We were both so taken with this extraordinary combination of motive power that we only had time for a passing greeting.

So, then, let me introduce Derek Cross. A farmer in Ayrshire who trained as a geologist. He has for several years been in the top flight of railway photographers, and we are all immensely grateful to him for the pleasure that his pictures have given us. Last time I saw him he was using a Rollei (obviously, farmers are doing well in Ayrshire!). By now, he may well have changed it for something else, as railway photographers tend to be restless with their apparatus.

It is, perhaps, rather presumptuous of me to introduce Derek Cross to the 'consumers' of this album of pictures. He needs no introduction: he is far too well known. He might just as well introduce me! The reason that I am involved in this book is that Ian Allan asked me to do a series of 'Roaming' books in the various regions of BR. I had to plead that there were certain areas that I could not adequately cover for lack of material. And so the suggestion was made that we should invite certain photographers to be responsible for books covering areas familiar to them. Derek Cross was the obvious choice for the railways north of the Border. As this book shows, he has some magnificent pictures of railways in the Scottish Region, and I am immensely grateful to him for agreeing to compile this book, especially as much of the work fell in harvest time.

Of railway books there seems no end. Inevitably there will be a good deal of repetition as the best view points are very quickly discovered by those with cameras. The pioneers of railway exploration, amongst whom I would number Derek Cross and myself, have to accept the fact that many of our favourite, and previously isolated, haunts have become common property. And, why not? We old stagers have no right to monopoly in this matter. It is for us, who have been at the game for a long time to bring to the light of day scenes which are no longer to be seen by the present day photographer; lines and stations that are no more, motive power depots that have been demolished, and engines throwing steam and smoke up into the sky. Let the younger folk do their best with the Diesels, the Electrics, and such preserved steam as they can stalk; we will show what it was like 30 years ago. It is because Derek Cross has presented pictures in this book which show the railway as it was, that it will be so acceptable to enthusiasts. There will be pictures of railway operation in the 1970s. This is good, as it will show the nature of the change that has taken place in the railway scene.

ERIC TREACY
(Editorial Adviser of the 'Roaming' Series)

Preface

O why do you walk through the fields in gloves,
Missing so much and so much?
O fat white woman whom nobody loves,
Why do you walk through the fields in gloves?

'To a Lady seen from a Train'

Frances Cornford never really answered this one, anymore than I can answer the inevitable 'Why do you photograph trains?' I suppose the slick answer would be because I like trains and don't particularly like people. Indeed there was a time, when it looked as though the steam locomotive would last for ever, that I never kept a negative of a train if somebody had their head looking out a window: the driver or firemen were allowed but little Willie, definitely no! It appals me now to think of the interesting negatives that went into the fire on account of this prejudice. Quite apart from the fascination of the steam locomotive two other factors have been dominant in my photographic career: first an interest in the railway as part of the landscape, a fact all too evident when I look at my photographic collection in bulk and second what might be called the 'hunter's instinct'. The latter is a case of myself against something that tends to have the advantage, the same applies to stalking and shooting where the quarry holds the cards. The steam engine certainly did as it had wind and weather on its side to blow smoke the wrong way at the vital moment or the Biblical 'small cloud' that came up at the last moment in the wrong place when you could perfectly well have sworn that it should have been heading in quite the opposite direction. When I started taking a serious interest in railway photography it was essentially a 'loner's' sport carried out far from the madding crowd. If I had wanted crowds I could have gone to a football match. Little did I realise how soon this was to change for in the middle 1960s one was liable to find more people at Shap Wells on a Saturday afternoon than at many football matches.

My landscape approach to railway photography can partly be accounted for by my professional training as a geologist but also a sense of wonder how the early railway engineers, with little more than picks and shovels and very primitive explosives, made such a good job of building our great main lines. Three men stand out in their ability to use every advantage offered by the terrain and at the same time leave it remarkably unscarred. These men were Locke, some of whose work on the Caledonian main line is illustrated in this book; Grainger who was responsible for the Edinburgh & Glasgow line and more dramatically, the Nithsdale route to Gretna and Mitchell whose original main line from Forres to Perth, considering the limited finances available and the nature of the terrain to be tackled, is probably the most remarkable in Britain. This in no way belittles the other Scottish railway engineers who did not have the same scope as the three I have mentioned because so many of what were to become important through lines in Scotland were built piecemeal, often with an eye to keeping somebody else out of that particular territory. Charles Foreman's West Highland, while a very remarkable feat of construction, was at heart a branch line and difficulties such as curvature and abrupt changes of grade were tolerated as there was never any intention of fast long distance non-stop running. The same is true of the Far North and Kyle Lines and much of the Great North of Scotland's system. One surprising fact that has emerged in researching for this book is the extraordinary lack of tunnels on the Scottish railway system especially considering the nature of the countryside to be tackled. The Highland got away with only two, both of them short, and the Far North, Kyle and West Highland lines had none at all if you discount a snow shed and an avalanche shelter!

To return to my photographic training I have to confess that this was conventional, starting with a folding 626 camera given to me at an early age by a distinguished jockey, no doubt with the idea that I might one day photograph racehorses and not the iron variety. In point of fact some of my early efforts did concern horses but also included friends and, to their disgust, relations and the family dogs of which there were many. This camera believe it or not had two shutter speeds apart from the hold-your-finger-on-the-button time exposure mechanism. These speeds were, if I remember correctly, 1/25th and 1/50th of a second; when at last it was explained to me that by using the latter I did not necessarily have to wait till the dog, horse or relation was standing still to get a picture, my career as a railway photographer was born. Mind you in these early days the use of a high shutter speed such as 1/50th needed a good deal of skill as while the hind legs and tail of the dog or horse might be in focus the rest was frequently missing, a lesson that had to be learned all over again when trains came in for consideration. Then came the war with all its unpleasant-nesses such as school and no film. It was only when things started to get back to normal that I took a photograph of a train, more or less by chance as a fishing expedition was not proving very profitable, and I had a crack at the old 3.40pm train from Stranraer to Dumfries on the Urr viaduct. Much to my surprise, it came out. After this I acquired some form of family heirloom in the form of a 116 folding Zeiss camera with the maximum shutter speed of 1/200th, on paper at any rate. In retrospect I doubt if it could have delivered half that speed but it was a big step forward. This machine had a bubble in a bath of oil above the viewfinder to show if you were holding the camera level, the snag being that while finding out, you couldn't see what you were taking. It also had a wooden base that was susceptible to humidity and if conditions were too humid things tended to be out of focus, still when everything was exactly right it gave reasonable results some of which are in this book. The Zeiss was a noble relic of a bygone era and when, some

years later, the termites had its wooden base for breakfast I was genuinely sorry.

Mention of this camera makes one realise just how far and how fast things have changed in the photographic world from ortho film or plates to the modern high speed films of today, from black and white to colour. Above all, there has been the rise of the 35mm camera with its vast range of reasonably-priced lenses, not that I have ever been an addict of this format for black and white photography but quite early on in the days of Dufaycolor, I managed to get some tolerable results with a second-hand Leica. After the demise of the Zeiss I used a folding 120 Agfa Record and got excellent results from it. While working as a geologist in the Pacific region, however, I found that I had to do a good deal of technical photography in the way of rock formations, landforms, vol-canoes, and the like so I invested in a Linhof Technika which, though considered light by press camera standards, was still a bulky brute to cart about along with spares, lenses etc. Geological work apart it proved ideal for railway photography being relatively easy to use, utterly reliable and nearly indestructible and what was more its max 1/500th shutter speed was very nearly what it claimed to be and this was enough for steam and diesel days though the LMR electrics beat it. With the end of steam I changed this for the Rollei 66 which, while handier to carry about than the Linhof and with a brilliant lens for colour work, I find more temperamental than the latter, especially when it comes to changing backs in a hurry.

When I was approached to do a photographic book on 'Roaming the Scottish Rails' my first reaction was one of horror. There may not be as many Scottish rails as there are English ones but they tend to be very spread out and Wick to Stranraer is a very long way with many miles containing very few trains. Added to this, the parts that I knew best in the south-west and centre of the country had been roamed over before by many more distinguished photographers than I. Apart from the problem of a fair geographical distribution which in the end was impossible to achieve, there was the other one of keeping out of other photographers' way, and to a certain extent my own for I am sure that by now people must think that I built the Pinmore viaduct or the Clyde Bridge at Crawford with my own hands! Before returning from abroad in 1960 I had virtually nothing north of Perth apart from some early efforts round Inverness. To an extent, however, I was saved by the instruction that the book was to contain some examples of modern traction, such as diesels and electrics. Here again it was not as simple as it seemed for I have come to the conclusion that the best way of photographing diesels is in colour, especially on such scenic lines as those to Kyle and Fort William so my black and white material in the North was sparse and much of that station shots, thanks to the Scottish Region's generosity in allowing me a series of cab trips over these isolated lines. One area however I am defeated by — the north-east, partly as I seldom had any reason for going there, and partly that by the time I came to live in Scotland steam had virtually gone from there. While a diesel in pleasant surroundings can make an attractive picture, I find that dmus, even white ones, defy all efforts to make them interesting. Given these limitations I have taken the term 'roaming' in the title as widely as I can to include several remote and rare branches such as that to Garlieston and the little known Cairn Valley line, where I found a shot of the demolition train that must have been taken about 1949 in the Zeiss days. That it was a sharp negative was partly due to the fact that demolition operations and the train had stopped for lunch!

It is remarkable how much of a collection of photographs taken over a mere 20 years (in Britain anyhow) should now have considerable historical interest. As an example of this when the Class 40 diesels started coming to the West Coast main line for most of a year it was a toss up whether such trains as the 'Royal Scot' and the Birmingham 'Scotsman' would be steam or diesel worked and mighty was the cursing if a diesel came instead of a 'Duchess'. Fifteen years later if a Class 40 appeared on the 'Scot' today while maybe not sending us into ecstasies it would be an event of note and makes one furious to think why we did not take more diesels while they were there. The same is true on lines about to be monopolised by that 'ton-up tadpole', the HST. The Scottish Region were lucky in that stroke of genius by the then general manager, James Ness, when the four pre-grouping engines were restored for an Indian summer of excursion workings. Some of them figure largely in this book and for which I make no apologies as they are all interred in the Glasgow Museum. They are unlikely to be seen in steam again despite an imaginative but, alas, abortive effort to make a film some three years ago based on the Race to Aberdeen, when, with a bit of cheating, the Caley Single might have reappeared. This book is very much one man's experience of roaming the Scottish rails. Much of the fascination of lonely signal boxes at dawn and the railwaymen I have met, many of who considered I was quite mad but were very nice about it, cannot be illustrated but it was tremendous fun... and still is at times such as when a long excursion hauled by two diesels came snaking down Loch Carron in bright sunshine, seconds ahead of a mountain storm. Not that one is always as lucky. I dare say if we were, we would all give up.

The Debatable Lands

For many hundreds of years, going back to Roman times and beyond, the Anglo-Scottish border has been fought over. Varying in location from century to century it was nowhere less defined than on the flat plains at the head of the Solway Firth created by the alluvial debris brought down from the hills by the two great rivers, the Esk and the Eden, a process which still continues to this day. The Romans made the first attempt to stabilise the border by building Hadrian's Wall and, very logically, following the natural line of the Tyne Gap from near Newcastle, up the Tyne Valley then over the watershed near Haltwhistle, and down to the alluvial lowlands of Cumbria. It is significant that the last major fort on the Wall was built on the north bank of the Eden not very far from Kingmoor near Carlisle. With the end of Roman occupation the border again became flexible as first one side then the other extended its territory north or south of the Eden/Esk basin. Partly on account of these sporadic wars and partly on account of its natural strategic location on the main trade routes between Scotland and the south, Carlisle grew in importance first as a fortified oasis then as a centre of trading.

With the coming of railways Carlisle became of crucial importance in communications between Lancashire and the south and Scotland because of the number of river valleys converging on the head of the Solway. Strange to relate, however, the two main ones, the Eden and the Esk, did not figure in the earliest railways of the district. At one time the Eden was considered by the Lancaster and Carlisle Railway before a final decision was made to build the line over Shap. The first two to be used were the valleys of relatively small rivers, the Petterill and the Caldew both of which, coming from the south, joined the Eden in Carlisle itself. The Petterill was followed from Penrith by the Lancaster and Carlisle, to become the LNW main line from the south. The Caldew was followed by the Maryport and Carlisle. The great Midland, Settle and Carlisle followed the Eden and its ally, the North British followed the Esk/Liddle Valleys. North of the Border the two main lines followed river valleys that entered the Solway west of the Eden/Esk complex. The Caledonian ran up the Annan Valley and Evan Water to the summit, and the Glasgow & South Western ran up the Nith Valley on an easier but more circuitous route by Dumfries. There is thus no doubt of the historical and geographical importance of Carlisle as a railway centre and as the essential starting point — despite the fact that it is in England — for any book covering the railways of Scotland.

My first short section thus covers this area of 'Debatable Lands' between Carlisle and Gretna. Though scenically uninspiring, it contains a wealth of railway interest which has changed widely over the past twenty years. The most important change has been the building of the vast new marshalling yard at Kingmoor and closure of the many smaller yards which caused endless congestion about the city in earlier times. Co-incident with the opening of Kingmoor New Yard came the gradual run down of steam which resulted in the closing of the loco depots at Durranhill (the old Midland Shed) Upperby and Canal (the LNER shed serving the Waverley Route and Newcastle lines) and, ultimately, the closing of the Waverley route itself and its branch to Silloth in the mid 1960s. This left as the only line to the north the old Caledonian route running flat and nearly straight from Citadel station to Gretna Junction. (Throughout the pre-grouping era the G&SW trains had running powers over it from Gretna.) The Waverley route also had a level run out to Longtown but by no means as straight, starting out to the west of the Caledonian line then crossing it at Kingmoor before bending north again.

Because of the flatness of the terrain there were few major earthworks other than some cuttings at Rockcliffe and the long embankment north of the Esk viaduct at Mossband on which the

Mossband troughs were sited. The major engineering works consisted of two great viaducts over the Eden at Etterby and the Esk at Metalbridge. Both these were typically Caledonian, plate girders on massive stone piers and both altered during and since the war. The main line structure at Etterby remains original but with a precast concrete structure to carry the goods lines on the west side obscuring the original. This new bridge was built during the war in a remarkably short time when congestion at Carlisle was at its worst. The longer viaduct over the Esk at Mossband was replaced by a concrete structure and widened to take three tracks in conjunction with the opening of Kingmoor yard in the early 1960s, much to the detriment of its appearance. The shorter structure, over the Sark Water that actually forms the border, is again typical Caledonian. The main lines remained double track apart from a mile from Dentonholme Junction to Kingmoor yard and approx another mile up to Floriston crossing where the up and down goods lines from Kingmoor yard join the fast lines. Beyond Floriston there is a third track on the up side as far as the entrance to the vast Ordnance Depot at the site of the old Mossband signal box. There were three stations on this length, Gretna Junction, Floriston and Rockcliffe all of which were closed after the war and have subsequently been demolished with the coming of electrification. Such are the approaches to Scotland from the Border City — a flat but interesting 8½ miles, booked to take between 7 and 7½ minutes start to pass by today's electrics.

Right: Carlisle station on 26 August 1967 with 'Jubilee' No 45562 *Alberta* on the Saturday-morning Leeds- Glasgow relief express being passed by Class 5 No 45285 arriving with a Glasgow- Blackpool train. No 45562 was one of the two 'Jubilees' kept in immaculate condition by Holbeck Shed (Leeds) for working relief expresses over the Settle & Carlisle line throughout the summer of 1967.

Top left: Two generations of motive power in Citadel station (Carlisle) on 5 August 1967. Peak Class diesel No D23 arrives with the 9.25am Leeds-Glasgow express while Class 5 No 44857 waits in the centre road to take over the following relief train.

Bottom left: The north-end of Carlisle station in August 1950. B1 No 61221 *Sir Alexander Erskine-Hill* pulls out with a Carlisle-Edinburgh train via the Waverley Route while 'Duchess' Pacific No 46232 *Duchess of Montrose* waits to the west of the signal box to take over an express off the West Coast main line.

Above: A line of locomotives at the north end of Kingmoor shed, coaled and watered ready to work north. Nos 45573 *Newfoundland*, 72006 *Clan Mackenzie* and an unidentified 'Black 5' on 15 May 1965.

Above: A far cry from the pristine standards of cleanliness once associated with Haymarket shed. A4 No 60012 *Commonwealth of Australia* crosses the marshy flats at Rockcliffe with a fitted freight from Edinburgh to Kingmoor Yard on 3 August 1963.

Top right: One of the features of the end of the Glasgow Fair fortnight was the working south of lengthy trains of empty stock on the Saturday evening. Rockcliffe again is the setting for A3 No 60070 *Gladiateur* with one such train from Corkerhill (Glasgow) to Leeds in July 1963.

Bottom right: V2 No 60957 overflows its tender on Mossband troughs in August 1958 while working the afternoon Perth-Euston express. At the time LNER engines frequently appeared on these turns as far as Carlisle.

Below: The down 'Royal Scot' crossing the viaduct over the River Esk in 1958 behind the last LMS Pacific No 46257 *City of Salford*. Many people are under the impression that the Esk is the Border between England and Scotland. In fact it is the very much smaller River Sark, a mile to the north. This viaduct very typical of the Caledonian, with stone piers and metal girders has now been replaced by an all-concrete structure.

Below: 'Jubilee' No 45718 *Dreadnought* crossing the River Sark at Gretna Junction with a parcels train for the Nith Valley line in 1961. The signs denoting the Border just visible to the right of the train.

Right: The down morning 'Caledonian' express takes the Caledonian main line at Gretna Junction in August 1958 behind No 46231 *Duchess of Atholl*. Gretna Junction signal box just visible above the third coach. The locomotive is in BR green livery (which in my opinion never suited the big LMS Pacifics) but beautifully clean as were all the engines rostered on this short-lived train.

Below: 'Britannia' No 70049, appropriately named *Solway Firth* in view of the location, curves sharply on to the Nith Valley line at Gretna Junction with a Saturdays-only relief train from Leeds to Glasgow in the summer of 1964.

The Caledonian Line from Gretna Junction ~ Glasgow

This is a typically Locke line — as straight as possible, no tunnels apart from one or two short ones on the environs of Glasgow, and has great similarities to his route for the Lancaster & Carlisle over Shap with its summit point in the middle and the approaches from the south undulating before a very steep final climb. In both cases the climbs from the north while not as spectacular are harder as they start almost from the terminus. Although not as steep they are longer. In the case of the Caledonian line, however, there is a breather of a few miles between Craigenhill Summit and Lamington where the line undulates along one of the flatter stretches of the Clyde Valley. Remarkably for a line reaching an altitude of 1,015ft, there are relatively few major earthworks other than some long but low cuttings in the Lockerbie area and the short high rock one immediately south of Beattock Summit. There are also several long embankments on the climb to Beattock from the south but Locke's superb eye for using a landscape has kept earthworks to a minimum. The main interest again lies in the viaducts which, with two exceptions are typical Caledonian girder on stone bases such as that over the Annan near Wamphray and those over the Clyde at Crawford and Lamington. The crossing of the Clyde south of Carstairs is exceptional in having bowstring girders instead of the more usual flat ones and the final crossing of the Clyde near Uddingston is very much higher than any of the others though this was not on the original line at all.

Between Gretna Junction and Beattock station the line undulates with a gradual rise to the north through relatively sheltered fertile country and no gradients steeper than 1 in 200. There must be nearly ten miles of this albeit broken by short lengths of level or descending line. At Beattock the scene changes with the erstwhile short branch to Moffat bearing eastwards to follow the Annan Valley. The main line continues due north up the valley of the Evan Water with the hills gradually closing in and the gradients gradually steepening from 1 in 88 to a final 1 in 74 to the summit over a distance of exactly ten miles. The climb to Beattock is worth a close look from both a geographical and engineering point of view. Even more than on the climb to Shap, Locke has used every aid that the landscape could give him and yet produced a line with no severe curvature and, considering the nature of the countryside, relatively little curvature at all. The result is that Beattock Bank while a hard slog going up, is a very fast run down. Even towards the end of steam three figure speeds were not unheard of (other than by Authority in Glasgow as there was a 90mph limit on the line). For three quarters of the way up the hill the line follows the sheltered western side of the ever-narrowing valley and as a result was largely free of snow trouble other than in the severest winter. Even then it was confined to the last two miles where the line crossed to the east of the valley above Harthope farm, again on a typical stone and girder viaduct.

Once over the summit the character of the line changes and the section from the Summit box to Crawford is the most open and bleakest of the whole line and is prone to snow trouble. After the first crossing of the Clyde at Crawford the whole nature of the countryside changes again as the line curves through Abington and on to Lamington, never far from the river and with a background of rolling hills dominated by the conical peak of Tinto to the west. Throughout the descent from Abington to the second crossing of the Clyde at Lamington increasingly more trees appear. In my opinion this is the most attractive length of the whole 102 miles. After Lamington the valley widens out and the river runs east of the line. Symington was once the junction for a branch through the hills to Peebles that shortly after the war was cut back to Broughton and is now closed completely. Carstairs, 73 miles from Carlisle, is an important junction with the line to Mid-Calder and Edinburgh and yet another crossing of the Clyde. In steam days there was the second set of water troughs at Stawfrank half a mile south of Carstairs station. At Carstairs the line bends northwestwards with a short sharp climb to Craigenhill and the start of the final descent to Glasgow through scenery ever more drab and industrial. The electrification of the suburban services as far as Lanark has reprieved most of the stations on this final section but, apart from Carstairs and Lockerbie, there are now no intermediate stations between Carlisle and Lanark Junction.

When the main line electrification came, Scottish Region were quite ruthless in blotting out all sign of these old stations, yards and signal boxes which seems a pity as many of the stations, especially in the Clyde Valley, were architecturally most attractive. The whole line is now controlled by two power boxes, one at Motherwell and one at Carlisle. In fairness, however, it must be said, that when boxes and stations were demolished the sites were cleared completely, levelled and grassed over. Loops remain at Abington, Summit, Beattock and Lockerbie but only the latter station now has any freight facilities. These changes have undoubtedly produced a very efficient high speed railway over relatively difficult terrain but with no branches between Gretna and

Carstairs it is somewhat featureless and even someone who knows the line well has difficulty in knowing exactly where they are. Apart from the lines to Glasgow Central, an electrified arm extends from Motherwell to Mossend yard, on the south-east side of Glasgow, which is now the main goods yard for the south and also the point where trains from London to Perth and beyond change from electric to diesel power.

Such then is the story of the Caledonian main line from its turbulent beginnings amid endless squabbling over routes through to the apparently clinical efficiency of today. Even now the scenery is set for another change as virtually the whole area between Beattock Summit and Elvanfoot has been planted with coniferous trees. Such plantations were a serious fire risk in days of steam but electrification has changed that just as it has changed the methods of signalling and track maintenance. For all its efficiency, however, I can't help wondering what will happen if a bad blizzard hits the exposed electrified sections on a winter's night, blocking points into and out of the various loops and possibly bringing down the wires. In steam days there were always surfacemen reasonably handy to turn out with shovels but not any more and it is a long way from Carstairs to Summit on a night of driving snow.

23

cclefechan

Above: Class 37 No D6853 pressed into service with a Blackpool-Glasgow relief train on Saturday 17 July 1971. To cope with the heavy Glasgow holiday traffic the Caledonian line, which at this time was normally closed during the day for electrification work, was specially reopened.

Top right: On most Sundays in the latter half of 1964 the G&SW line was closed to allow relining of the Drumlanrigg tunnel and traffic was diverted by way of Beattock. One interesting outcome of this was the afternoon Dumfries-Perth milk train which worked from Dumfries to Lockerbie over the single track branch through Lochmaben and produced a varied collection of motive power including on one occasion, an A1. This particular Sunday finds 'Britannia' No 70037 *Hereward the Wake*, joining the main line at Lockerbie off the branch.

Bottom right: The Jones Goods 4-6-0 ex-Highland Railway No 103 passing Beattock South box with an enthusiasts' special in October 1965 on what transpired to be its last public appearance in steam. One of Beattock's bankers, a Fairburn 2-6-4T, takes water in the background.

Above: 'Princess' No 46203 *Princess Margaret Rose* restarts the morning Euston-Perth express from Beattock station after taking banking assistance in August 1962. This was during the last six weeks that Kingmoor's three surviving 'Princesses' were regularly rostered on this train. They were kept in remarkably clean condition considering that their withdrawal was only weeks away.

Top right: Stranger at Beattock. A4 No 4498 *Sir Nigel Gresley* recently overhauled at Crewe and repainted in LNER livery at the north end of Beattock station with the late afternoon Carlisle-Perth parcels on 17 May 1967. The engine was to work a special out of Glasgow the following Saturday (See page 56) and Kingmoor made her earn her keep on the way north by working this train to Carstairs.

Bottom right: 'The Parly'. Old traditions died hard on the Caledonian and until the end of steam the 9am Carlisle-Glasgow stopping train was always known by this unofficial name, dating back to the days when it was a 'Parliamentary train'. Rebuilt 'Scot' No 46128 *The Lovat Scouts* at Auchencastle on the climb to Beattock Summit with the 'Parly' on a spring day in 1963.

Above: Greskine Box was half way up the 10 miles of Beattock bank and boasted a refuge siding occupied in this picture by B1 No 61308 with Train 6S61, a Kingmoor Yard-Edinburgh goods which during the last few years of steam was regularly worked by an ex-LNER locomotive as part of a cyclic diagram from Edinburgh-Newcastle-Carlisle and home via Carstairs. Class 40 No D307 overtakes with the morning Birmingham Scotsman' 25 July 1964.

Right: Strange goings on at Greskine. One of Beattock's bankers staggers towards the box deputising for a 'Britannia' that had failed in Beattock station with a Ripon-Rutherglen troop special on 25 July 1964. No 42214 was not in good shape and in turn was banked onwards from Greskine by Standard 2-6-0 No 76090 that had previously worked a short permanent way train to Summit and was returning to Beattock light engine.

Above: Early summer's morning above Greskine with an overnight Euston/Glasgow sleeper climbing towards Summit banked by one of the Fairburn 2-6-4Ts that were bankers at Beattock at this time.

Top right: No 46200 *The Princess Royal* in sparkling maroon livery attacking the final third of Beattock bank behind Harthope Farm with the morning Euston-Perth express again banked in a somewhat leisurely fashion by a Fairburn 2-6-4T. This photo taken in September 1962 marks the swan song of Kingmoor's 'Lizzies', all three being withdrawn at the end of that month.

Bottom right: Train 6S61 again — the afternoon Kingmoor-Edinburgh goods between Harthope and the summit cutting hauled by V2 No 60910. While B1s were the normal loco for this turn, V2s were used sometimes and, rarely, an A3 Pacific. Needless to say the only time I saw the latter it was pouring with rain!

Left: The morning Manchester-Glasgow train above Harthope on 8 July 1961 hauled by rebuilt 'Scot' No 46105 *Cameron Highlander* and double banked by Fairburn and Fowler 2-6-4 tanks Nos 42197 and 42301. Double banking on Beattock was not common and this is the only time I have ever seen a Fowler tank on such duties. Even more surprising was that this was the only trip it made all day and one explanation is that it was an engine displaced from the Glasgow suburban service working back to the LMR that Beattock took a turn out of in passing.

Above: The CTAC's Tours express from Manchester to Wemyss Bay passing under the original main road bridge a mile south of Beattock Summit on a scorching June day in 1963. It was so hot in fact that while 'Jubilee' No 45613 *Kenya* was working hard, there is not a trace of exhaust, very rare on Beattock.

Below: Fairburn 2-6-4T coasts through the high rock cutting half a mile south of Summit with the one coach 'Siege', another train with an unofficial name on the Caledonian main line. No 42214 with the Saturdays-only Summit to Moffat (latterly to Beattock) train run for the benefit of railwaymen's wives to do their weekend shopping and which stopped at all the cottages on the way down the bank. The origin of the name is obscure but probably arose as it first ran during the Siege of Mafeking though what this had to do with shopping trips to Beattock, I cannot think.

Below: The superbly elegant lines of the 'Princess' class are shown to perfection in this photo of the last of the Kingmoor trio. No 46201 *Princess Elizabeth* in very clean green livery tops Beattock Summit in August 1961 again with the morning Euston-Perth express which at this time carried a through portion for Aberdeen.

Top left: Beattock Summit signal box must have survived many icy blasts over the years but it failed to survive the trauma of electrification and is now replaced by a mundane board at the lineside. Summit box so very typical of many on the Caley main line forms the background to Class 5 No 44954 on an up parcels train in September 1961.

Bottom left: No 46226 *Duchess of Norfolk* makes light work of the climb from the north as she passes Summit with a heavy Perth-London express on 19 August 1961. Both up and down loops remain at Summit after electrification in somewhat modified form and are now controlled from the power box at Motherwell.

Above: Old places, new faces! Beattock Summit, post-electrification, early on an August morning in 1976 with Class 86/2 No 86 246 at the north end of the loops with train 1S05 Euston-Inverness sleeper running very late.

Above: Something of the bleakness of Elvanfoot is shown in this picture of Class 40 No D226 on the up 'Royal Scot' passing through the loop at Elvanfoot. It is overtaking a preceding Edinburgh-Liverpool train hauled by Class 5 No 44877 which had run short of steam on the main line at the start of the Edinburgh holiday fortnight in June 1964.

Top right: Two Class 5s Nos 44955 and 44903 show no signs of shortage of steam the same morning as they storm through Elvanfoot with an Edinburgh-Blackpool extra.

Bottom right: B1 No 61242 *Alexander Reith Gray* steams alongside the infant River Clyde a mile north of Elvanfoot with train 6S61 — the afternoon Kingmoor-Edinburgh goods with an ex-LNER loco in charge as usual.

Above: A very rare visitor to the Clyde Valley, an ex-North British J37 0-6-0 No 64581, climbs round the long curve between Abington and Crawford with an up goods train, presumably from Edinburgh to Carlisle, on a hot September day in 1961.

Top right: New look crossing the Clyde at Crawford. Class 87 No 87 009 hurtles northwards with a Glasgow-bound express shortly after electrification on 29 June 1974.

Bottom right: Class 86/2 No 86 236 a mile south of Abington on 29 June 1974 with a late afternoon Glasgow-Euston express. The winding stretch between here and Crawford is one of the few lengths of the old Caledonian main line where the maximum speed is limited to 90mph.

Top left: 'Britannia' No 70052 *Firth of Tay* leans to one of the many curves between Abington and Crawford with the morning Crewe-Perth train in April 1961. This photo shows the build up of smoke in front of the funnel a phenomenon shared with the 'Duchesses', especially if fired when coasting.

Bottom left: Typical scenery of the upper Clyde Valley forms the backdrop to No 46255 *City of Hereford* apparently taking things easy with the afternoon Aberdeen and Perth-Euston express on a hot August day in 1961. The white feather at the safey valves and the fireman looking out admiring the view indicate that the engine was steaming well on the last stages of the long climb from Carstairs to the Summit.

Above: Riddles-designed 'Austerity' 2-10-0, number unknown, with a southbound goods between Abington and Crawford in 1950. The ten-coupled 'Austerities', forerunners of the Standard 9Fs, were popular on the hilly lines of South Scotland whereas the eight-coupled variety most decidedly were not.

Below: The Saturdays-only 12.30pm stopping train from Glasgow to Lockerbie pulls out of the charming station at Abington under the charge of rebuilt 'Scot' No 46142 *The York & Lancaster Regiment*. This train which ran forward from Lockerbie to Carlisle empty stock was a regular turn for a big engine returning south despite its light load and leisurely ways. While the loops remain at Abington the station is demolished and in its place there is a electric sub-station which, aesthetically, is definitely not an improvement.

Below: The 'Parly' again. The 9am Carlisle-Glasgow stopping train skirts the Clyde near Wandel Mill between Abington and Lamington on a May morning in 1962 with 'Britannia' No 70051 *Firth of Forth* in charge.

Top left: The dip to the crossing of the Clyde at Lamington in steam days was always a place where drivers tried to gain a bit of impetus for the long climb to Beattock Summit. In April 1961 'Jubilee' No 45731 *Perseverance* and 'Duchess' No 46223 *Princess Alice* pile on steam after crossing the Clyde with the morning Glasgow and Edinburgh to Birmingham train which at certain times of the year regularly provided a piloted Pacific between Carstairs and Carlisle.

Bottom left: With Tinto Hill as a backdrop, No 46227 *Duchess of Devonshire* sweeps past Lamington and on to the Clyde viaduct with the Glasgow-Birmingham express on 7 September 1961.

Above: 'Clan' No 72000 *Clan Buchanan* emerges from the mist hanging about the river at Lamington with a northbound goods on a frosty March morning in 1961.

Top left: Like so many stations in the Clyde Valley now demolished with the coming of electrification, Lamington had a very distinctive rural charm set in the flat river valley of the Clyde and dominated by the flanks of Tinto. Class 40 No D306 passes through with the morning Glasgow–Manchester express in May 1964 by which time all the major West Coast trains had become diesel hauled... 10 years later the electrics had swept them away in their turn.

Bottom left: The River Clyde again forms the background to a northbound goods train between Wandel Mill and Lamington hauled by Standard 5 No 73063 in June 1962.

Above: The down Birmingham 'Scotsman' approaching Lamington in September 1950 hauled by No 46208 *Princess Helena Victoria*. Photos here are no longer possible as the scrub in the foreground is now 20ft high.

Below: A brace of Class 25s Nos D5202 and 5204 head northwards past Leggatfoot signal box with a Saturday extra from Blackpool to Paisley in August 1970, diverted from the Nith Valley line on account of a derailment at Carronbridge.

Below: At one time the branch from Symington on the main line extended to Peebles but when this picture was taken in September 1961 it terminated at Broughton and was freight-only serving mainly the meat works at Broughton. A Branch Line Society excursion leaves the terminus hauled by ex-Caledonian 0-4-4T No 55124.

Top left: Ex-Caley Class 60 No 54641 crossing the Clyde south of Carstairs with an up goods in September 1949. Known as 'Greybacks', the Caley 60s were not popular with anyone in South Scotland but nonetheless put in a lot of useful work on freight traffic into the early 1950s.

Bottom left: 'Jubilee' No 45727 *Inflexible* over-estimates its tank capacity on Strawfrank troughs south of Carstairs working the morning Liverpool-Glasgow express in June 1961. The photographer survived albeit somewhat wet!

Above: Diverted from its home territory on 23 June 1972 owing to bridge renewals at Dunbar, 'Deltic' No D9002 *The Kings Own Yorkshire Light Infantry* eases a Sunday morning Edinburgh-Kings Cross train round the curve on to the West Coast main line at Strawfrank Junction at the south end of the Carstairs triangle. Carstairs MPD and coaling tower visible in the background.

Above: The Euston-Perth train approaching Strawfrank Junction from the south on 29 August 1962 hauled by No 46203 *Princess Margaret Rose* during the last weeks of 'Princess'-working out of Carlisle. The sidings in the foreground served the PW depot at Carstairs and were to play a big part in the electrification of the Clyde Valley line before being removed.

Top right: 'Jubilee' No 45658 *Keyes* fires heavily passing under the gantry at the north end of Carstairs station with train 1M25, a relief to the up 'Royal Scot' in June 1963.

Bottom right: Class 50 No D433 passing under the Carstairs gantry with a short train from Perth to Carstairs on 15 August 1970. This train, apart from giving local service while the main trains were diverted for electrification work, was used as a crew training trip for the Perth men on Class 50s.

Right: The evening sun catches A2/3 Pacific No 60524 *Herringbone* on the final stretch of the climb to Craigenhill Summit with the Aberdeen portion of the up postal. The lights and pick up equipment so much a feature of the older TPO vehicles are very clearly visible.

Below: Glasgow Central, 20 May 1967. No 4498 *Sir Nigel Gresley* backs on to an A4 Society special for Perth and Aberdeen. Two days previously this engine had been used on the afternoon Carlisle-Perth parcels train between Carlisle and Carstairs (See page 27) at Beattock.

The Nith Valley Line and Branches Glasgow/Annan

This line, though very different in geographical character from the rival Caledonian, was also engineered by a man with an eye to using the land forms to the maximum advantage. Grainger, in building the Nith Valley line, however, had only one main valley to follow — that of the Nith from New Cumnock to Dumfries. The other main rivers, the Ayr and the Lugar, flowed westwards across his path as did many of the tributaries of the Nith coming down from the Lowther Hills to the east, often in steep ravines through the relatively soft New Red Sandstone rock. The result of this is that, while the Caledonian Line was relatively free of major earthworks, the most notable feature of the G&SW route is its many great viaducts. Almost all of them were built from stone quarried nearby, for the Red Sandstone of the river gorges was also a very good building stone, easy to work and, once weathered for a few years, very resistant to erosion. The original line to Kilmarnock followed the route from Glasgow to Ayr through Paisley as far as Dalry where it turned south-eastwards to climb gradually to Kilmarnock. The Dalry/Kilmarnock section is now closed which seems strange as the remaining 'Joint' line between Barrhead and Kilmarnock is the hardest stretch from a locomotive point of view of the whole route with heavy grades from Nitshill (just on the Glasgow side of Barrhead) to Shilford Summit with an equally hard climb from Kilmarnock to Dunlop. The reason for the line being known as 'Joint' was that it was owned by the G&SW and the Caledonian who had endless fun squabbling about who was to look after it.

Glasgow is left behind on the South West route far quicker than on the Caledonian. Once past Barrhead the line runs through open agricultural country with curves and cuttings abounding, especially on the initial climb from Barrhead to the Shilford. It also boasts, at Stewarton, the first of the great stone viaducts. It spans a wide valley which seems out of all proportion to the small steam at its bottom. In pre-grouping days Kilmarnock was the hub of the G&SW with the locomotive works and a multitude of branch lines to places such as Darvel, Ardrossan and Ayr. However, with the closure of all the branch lines and the run down in the coal and manufacturing industries, it is no longer as important as it once was. Some idea of the nature of the Nith Valley line can be gauged from the fact that till the mid-1950s it was not uncommon for expresses to be piloted from St Enoch to Kilmarnock then left to tackle the longer but less steep gradients to the south unaided. Immediately south of Kilmarnock are two more stone viaducts — one over the town and the other over the River Irvine near Hurlford. After crossing the latter the climb to the summit begins with five miles around 1 in 100 to Mossgiel tunnel followed by a short undulating stretch through Mauchline and over the Ballochmyle viaduct, the most dramatic of them all, with its great single span masonry arch over the River Ayr. Mauchline still remains an important junction where a very busy mineral line diverges to Ayr though, like all the Nith Valley stations between Kilmarnock and Dumfries except for Kirkconnel, it no longer has a passenger service.

South of Ballochmyle the climb continues on easier grades through the heart of the central Ayrshire coalfields to the summit of the line at Polquhap, 3½ miles south of Cumnock, through a series of short cuttings culminating in the half-mile long Blackfaulds Cutting immediately north of Polquhap, this has always been a terror in times of snow. It is an interesting point that the G&SW line, though nearer the coast and running at a lower altitude than the Caledonian, has been more prone to snow trouble, mainly on account of the cuttings on the high windswept Ayrshire plateau and the fact that it follows the eastern and more exposed side of Nithsdale. Beyond the summit there are several level stretches alongside the water meadows of the Nith round New Cumnock and the one and only set of water troughs in steam days at Upper Cairn. The Nith, like many Welsh rivers, is relatively flat at its source and mouth but steep through the middle sections. At Kirkconnel the coalfields are left behind and the really spectacular stretch begins with the valley becoming narrower. High steep hills on both sides culminate in the Drumlanrigg Gorge. It is here that viaduct follows viaduct as the line twists its way, clinging to the steep hillsides on the eastern side of the valley, before plunging into the Drumlanrigg tunnel. This tunnel is the longest on the line and also a very difficult one to maintain on account of the fractured nature of the rock it passes through. Carronbridge station at the east end of this tunnel marks the end of the gradual fall through the gorge and the start of 12 miles of steeper descent, much of it at 1 in 200, to beyond Auldgirth. Carronbridge also boasts another remarkable stone viaduct that not only has a break of grade in the middle but also starts to curve half way across. A delightful story about the building of this very high and complicated structure is still current in Dumfriesshire lore — the engineers were in a muddle and had to be sorted out by a passing tramp for the cost of a cup of tea... it is too improbable not to be true!

The last few miles from the crossing of the Nith at Portrack, near Auldgirth, into Dumfries are gently rolling. The approaches are marked by yet another sandstone viaduct which, unlike those to the north, is flat-arched as is its counterpart on the approach to Annan. Dumfries, up till 1965, was the junction for the 'Port Road', that lonely line serving Galloway and finishing up at Stranraer, and also for a branch to Lockerbie built by the hated Caledonian who, at one time, had their own station at Dumfries. Beyond Dumfries, apart

from a slight rise between Racks and Ruthwell, the line is very gently undulating with no engineering features of note. Between Annan and Gretna Junction it has been singled and is controlled by the new power box at Carlisle. Compared with the electrified line over Beattock, the Nith Valley has a lot of the charm of the past about it. Though most of the stations are closed, they remain in situ along with many of the signal boxes and the length from Auldgirth to Sanquhar must rate as one of the most scenic in Scotland. Undoubtedly the Nith Valley's finest hours came during the Caledonian electrification works when all the daytime trains between England and the north were routed that way. After this there have been repeated rumours of its pending closure but heavy freight traffic between the NE of England and the Ayrshire coast and the possibility of the development of Hunterston as a deep water harbour have saved it so far. The future also looks reasonably secure, especially as it has proved very useful as a diversionary route, on one occasion carrying both East and West Coast traffic when derailments at Grantshouse and Wamphray blocked both other lines simultaneously.

Ironically shortly before correcting the proofs of this book, the Nith Valley again came into its own as the only through route between Glasgow and Carlisle, when the last weekend of October 1977 brought storms and torrential rain over the whole of south Scotland. Not only did the gale force winds bring down several lengths of electric overheads, but floods washed away nearly half a mile of the Caledonian line near Wamphray. For three days all the services between London and the North had to be diverted through Dumfries and Kilmarnock.

Top left: St Enoch station in happier days. 'Duchess' No 46244 *King George VI* pulls out with the 5.30pm semi-fast train to Carlisle, the descendant of a post-war train to Plymouth which produced one of the first regular Pacific workings over the G&SW route. The four local coaches in front of this train were detached at Kilmarnock.

Bottom left: The G&SW route to Greenock was a very busy line at the time of the great races between the steamers of the rival railway companies plying on the Clyde. After the war decline set in and beyond Kilmacolm the line was used only for the odd boat-train and excursion traffic such as this train returning from the annual Orangewalk parades in Greenock, seen crossing the viaduct behind Upper Port Glasgow on 6 July 1963 with Standard tank No 80059 piloting Standard Mogul No 76094.

Above: The line that became the main line between Glasgow and Kilmarnock was joint between the Caley and the G&SW and to this day is known as the 'Joint Line' to the locals. The heaviest part of the climb from south Glasgow to the Ayrshire plateau was the Neilston Bank, tackled here by the up 'Thames-Clyde' express in April 1961 hauled by A3 No 60036 *Colombo* in one of the A3s least-pleasing forms with double chimney but no smoke deflectors.

Top left: The Caledonian influence on the Joint line is evident in the buildings and layout of Caldwell station playing host to a passing Euston-Glasgow sleeping car express behind No 46232 *Duchess of Montrose*, 5 June 1962.

Bottom left: One of the features of the Nith Valley line was the multitude of great stone viaducts. Here No 46226 *Duchess of Norfolk* crosses to northernmost of these structures near Stewarton with a Dover-Glasgow school special on an April morning in 1963.

Above: Another rural station on the 'Joint Line' at Kilmaurs which shows more G&SW influence in architecture and layout. A relief to the up 'Thames-Clyde' express passes Kilmaurs on 30 March 1964 behind Class 5 No 45171 piloting 'Jubilee' No 45608 *Gibraltar*.

Top left: The original G&SW line between Kilmarnock and Glasgow ran by way of Dalry and Paisley. A London-Glasgow express diverted by way of this line owing to engineering work approaches Dalry Junction hauled by Class 50 No D415 on 23 July 1973.

Bottom left: In its heyday, Kilmarnock was the hub of the G&SW sitting like a spider in the midst of a web of branches which one by one have closed and Kilmarnock's importance has dwindled accordingly. In August 1963 however Pacifics still graced its platforms as in this photo of A3 No 60071 *Tranquil* leaving with a Leeds-Glasgow relief express.

Above: During the electrification of the Caledonian line the Nith Valley became very busy with diversions such as 1M30, the descendant of the 'Midday Scot', heading south through Kilmarnock station with Nos D445 and 410 in charge.

Top left: Winter sunshine and steam at Kilmarnock as B1 No 61278 makes a water stop with a Branch Line Society excursion from Glasgow to Carlisle and back by the Waverley Route shortly before the latter closed.

Bottom left: The second hard climb for southbound trains on the Nith Valley route began at Hurlford to the Mossgiel tunnel near Mauchline. Here on the steepest part of this climb near Garrochburn sidings 'Clan' No 72007 *Clan Mackintosh* puts up a stirring performance with the 5.30pm St Enoch-Carlisle in July 1964.

Above: No 45739 *Ulster* lifts a relief to the up 'Thames-Clyde' express past Garrochburn signal box which was the junction for an NCB line serving Mauchline Colliery.

Above: Standard Class 4 Mogul No 76091 at Garrochburn with a rake of empty wagons for Bank Junction near New Cumnock. The sidings in the background at one time were used for loading clay from a nearby opencast working.

Top right: Mauchline is the junction for the lines from the south to Kilmarnock and Ayr respectively. Class 5 No 44783 takes the main line with a Glasgow stopping train in 1961 while 'Crab' No 42745 pulls out on to the branch for Ayr with a load of coal from Barony Colliery.

Bottom right: Hurlford's Class 5 No 45124 might have been nice and clean but was not steaming well this May morning with a Kilmarnock-Blackpool excursion and stopped for assistance from 'Crab' No 42780, commandeered off a mineral train for Ayr. Here the ill-assorted pair leave Mauchline for the south, the pilot presumably being detached at New Cumnock.

Top left: North of Mauchline in 1950 as 2P No 40661 returns to Hurlford with the breakdown train. The lines to Ayr diverging in the foreground.

Bottom left: The Ballochmyle viaduct south of Mauchline has the largest single stone arch of any bridge in Britain and possibly in the world. Some idea of the size and grace of this span is shown in this early spring morning photo in 1963 with the vast structure dwarfing rebuilt 'Scot' No 46157 *The Royal Artilleryman* on an overnight St Pancras to Glasgow sleeping car train.

Above: The batch of B1s that came to Ayr in the early 1960s had a mixed reception being considered deficient in brake power for the harder goods turns. However, they were used on easier jobs such as the daily Ayr/Catrine goods seen here near Brackenhill Junction in April 1964 with No 61261 shortly before the closure of the branch.

Above: A1 No 60131 *Osprey* with a southbound goods at Brackenhill Junction. The date 27 July 1964 and the branch to Catrine visible in the background. Ex-LNER Pacifics worked extras north on Saturdays and their return workings as far as Carlisle were always interesting, varying from stopping passenger trains to the one van Kilmarnock-Dumfries paper train on Monday mornings.

Above: Standard 5 No 73100 waits at
Catrine station with the daily goods for Ayr in
April 1964 shortly before this short but
steeply graded branch was closed.

Above: A sad sight at Auchinleck in March 1965. Rebuilt 'Scot' No 46155 *The Lancer* and rebuilt 'Patriot' No 45527 *Southport* head for the West of Scotland ship-breaking yard at Troon behind Class 5 No 44955 after their withdrawal from Upperby shed (Carlisle). Upperby shed (Carlisle).

Top right: Ex-Caledonian 2F 0-6-0 No 57331 creeps to a stop at Gilminscroft sidings near Auchinleck with a goods train off the branch to Muirkirk in 1961 by which time Ayrshire's once numerous Caley 2s were getting very thin on the ground.

Bottom right: No 72005 *Clan Macgregor* crosses the Templin viaduct near Cumnock on 28 April 1962 with an up parcels train. This viaduct, so typical of the line, was built from local stone quarried nearby which was a feature of nearly all the G&SW viaducts including Ballochmyle.

Below: Polquhap, though nearly 400ft lower than Beattock, was nearly as bleak and, approached from the north by the long, rocky Blackfaulds cutting, notorious for snow blocks in severe weather. No 46223 *Princess Alice* entering this cutting at the Cumnock end with the 5.30pm Glasgow (St Enoch)–Carlisle in July 1963.

Below: The line opens out again in the south end of Blackfaulds cutting for a final easy mile to Polquhap. On a damp day in April 1964 No 72005 *Clan Macgregor* makes heavy weather of the final climb out of Blackfaulds with an Easter Monday relief to the up 'Thames-Clyde' express.

Top left: A southbound ballast train passing under the main A76 road bridge near the summit hauled by 'Crab' No 42911 in April 1961.

Bottom left: The 11.40pm Euston-Glasgow sleeping car express sweeps round the long curve immediately north of Polquhap box (just out of sight) on a frosty April morning in 1951. 'Duchess' No 46220 *Coronation* piloted by a Class 5 No 44899 at a time when this train was regularly piloted, partly on account of its weight, and partly to balance engine workings. The pilot is still fitted with the small snow plough common to many Scottish Region engines in winter.

Above: Caley 3F 0-6-0 No 57601 storms past New Cumnock station in 1963 with a coal train from Kirkconnel to Ayr Harbour. With the closing of several mines in South Ayrshire this traffic has ceased.

Below: Yet another of the graceful G&SW
viaducts this time over the Crawick Water a
mile north of Sanquhar. The train, is the
morning Leeds-Glasgow hauled by
Class 45 No D16 on 25 September 1971.

Top left: Undoubtedly the most scenic part of the G&SW is the run through the Drumlanrigg Gorge between Sanquhar and Thornhill where both railway and road squeeze between the high hills to the east and the River Nith. Class 5 No 45194 in the gorge near Enterkinefoot on 4 July 1964 with the Saturdays-only Heads of Ayr-Newcastle train.

Bottom left: Class 5 No 44662 in the Drumlanrigg Gorge on Saturday 4 July 1964 with the morning Blackpool-Glasgow train passing under the steep escarpment known locally as 'the Priest's Crown'.

Above: The Carronbridge viaduct — after Ballochmyle probably the highest and most spectacular on the line. It posed considerable problems in its construction because it starts to curve and descend half way across. Standard 5 No 73062 with a Manchester-Glasgow relief train on 4 July 1964.

Above: While the electrification of the Caledonian route over Beattock was in progress, all the daytime trains from Glasgow to the south ran via the Nith Valley. One of these, the 4pm Glasgow-Euston, is hauled by Class 50s Nos D404 and 418 in multiple near Closeburn on 17 July 1971.

Top right: 'The line that never was' might well describe the Cairn Valley light railway from Dumfries to Moniaive. Virtually unknown outside the immediate area, it has seldom ever been photographed and I was delighted to come across this photo of the demolition train on the branch near Dunscore about 1949, hauled by an unidentified Caley 2F.

Bottom right: No 4472 *Flying Scotsman* takes the Lochmaben branch to Lockerbie at the north end of Dumfries station with a Gainsborough Model Railway Society excursion of 15 May 1965. This line was built by the Caledonian and terminated at St Mary's station in Dumfries, latterly a goods yard just visible above the A3s tender. The train at this point is on the connecting spur with the G&SW line.

Below: Dumfries shed in April 1965. A1 No 60154 *Bon Accord* and Class 5 No 45013. The A1 had worked a relief train to Glasgow on the Saturday and was on its way back to Carlisle in stages, the first of which had been the Glasgow-Dumfries paper train. Here it waits to continue with a fitted van train from the Metal Box Factory near Dumfries to Kingmoor Yard (Carlisle).

Below: Standard Tank No 80117 pulls out of Dumfries with a short train for Stranraer shortly before the closure of the 'Port Road' to Stranraer in 1965. The original 'Lighthouse' signal box clearly visible on the hill in the background, now demolished in an act of planning vandalism.

Above: Stanier 3PT No 40152 eases a train from Kirkcudbright into Dumfries in 1961 when two of these engines were shedded at Dumfries. The main line to the north in the background.

Top right: Passing the site of Lochanhead station 10 miles west of Dumfries 'Jubilee' No 45629 *Straits Settlements* pilots Class 5 No 44791 with the empty stock of a Newcastle-Castle Douglas excursion on 27 May 1964.

Bottom right: Early morning at Annan in 1964 as Standard Class 2MT No 78051 does some steamy shunting with the Dumfries-Carlisle Goods while Standard 5 No 73098 makes a slippery start with a Glasgow-bound parcels.

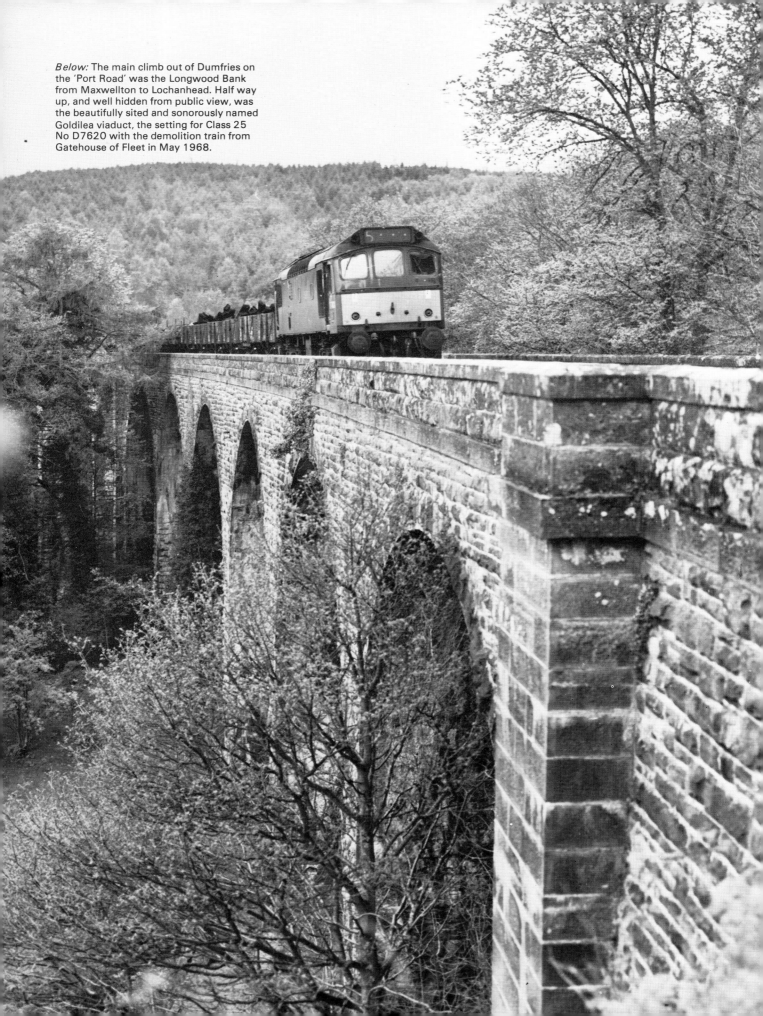

Below: The main climb out of Dumfries on the 'Port Road' was the Longwood Bank from Maxwellton to Lochanhead. Half way up, and well hidden from public view, was the beautifully sited and sonorously named Goldilea viaduct, the setting for Class 25 No D7620 with the demolition train from Gatehouse of Fleet in May 1968.

Edinburgh, the East Coast and Waverley Routes

Edinburgh — the tourist trap of Scotland, set in a superb situation with some splendid architecture and on Sunday afternoons all the animation of a disused film-set. Scotland's capital used to boast three main railway stations. They ranged from the somnolant opulence of the Caledonian's Princes Street, through the chaotic bustle of Waverley, not without charm certainly, but a charm more in its setting than its design, to the dingy squalor of Haymarket which to this day might be held up as an example of all that was bad in North British railway architecture. Princes Street was closed in 1965 and its sparse traffic diverted by way of a spur to Haymarket and Waverley, adding its mite to the chaos at the latter which, in my memories of steam days, with several branch lines still open, could be very great indeed. Now, however, with all but one of the local services withdrawn and diesel traction requiring fewer light engine movements, not to mention the extensive use of dmus and the Edinburgh/Glasgow pull and push services, Waverley is a quieter, more ordered place than in days of yore. It is also a highly photogenic station both in itself and its western approaches through Princes Street gardens, a fact greatly appreciated by railway enthusiasts but not by the natives who maintained that nasty dirty steam trains sullied their fair city. I have used a picture in this book to prove their point.

Two main lines to the south used Waverley before the closure of Princes Street station, the East Coast main line by way of Dunbar to Berwick-on-Tweed and the Waverley Route over the hills to Hawick and Carlisle. Both these lines were built and owned by the North British Company but for a long time the North Eastern had the idea that it should work most, if not all of the long distance expresses right through from Newcastle to Edinburgh. Great was the ill feeling engendered thereby. However, as both railways came within the compass of the LNER at the grouping, things settled down amicably enough and it is to the East Coast route that I turn first. The start out of Waverley is a steep descent through a tunnel and cuttings at 1 in 78 for a mile and a half to St Margarets, site of one of the two loco depots servicing Waverley. It could be a nasty climb for heavy trains at the end of a long run from the south. Thereafter the line undulated very gently through the market gardening lands of the Lothian coast as far as Dunbar, the main feature of the first six miles out of Edinburgh being the number of junctions: Portobello for the Waverley route and lines into Leith; New Hailes for the defunct branch to Musselburgh and finally Monktonhall which, if anything, has grown in importance with the opening of the marshalling yard at Millerhill. Beyond Monktonhall there was a junction at Longniddry for Haddington and a mile beyond at Aberlady Junction for Gullane, both branches now closed and lifted. Finally there was one at Drem for North Berwick which still remains as Edinburgh's only local service to the east.

South of Dunbar the scene changes as the line climbs to a summit at Penmanshiel tunnel on gradients as steep as 1 in 96 for four miles through Cockburnspath. Once over the top the line drops steadily to Berwick-on-Tweed. The first few miles run through the valley of the Eye Water which, after a cloudburst, turned into a raging spate in 1948 destroying several bridges and closing the main line for weeks. There were two more branches in the last miles to Berwick-on-Tweed, one for Duns going off at Reston, and the other for Eyemouth, both now closed. The five miles from Burnmouth to Berwick have some tantalising glimpses of the North Sea which are the most memorable scenic features on an otherwise relatively featureless line. The border is crossed, not as many suppose by the Royal Border Bridge over the Tweed at Berwick, but at a place called Marshall Meadows two miles to the north with the line in sight of the sea to the east and of a positively repulsive caravan site to the west.

If the East Coast main line is flat and featureless, the Waverley Route was anything but. Right from the junction at Portobello it started climbing, gradually at first past the new Millerhill Yard and Eskbank to Hardengreen Junction, but from here the next 9 miles to Falahill Summit was a killer, being mostly on a grade of 1 in 70 and abounding in curves — the most spectacular, the great semi-circle above the ruins of Borthwick Castle. The Waverley Route was a line of contrasts as the first part of the climb passed through the heart of the Lothians coalfield. The rest passed through ever wilder and bleaker country to Tynehead and the lonely loops and box at Falahill. From this point the line dropped steadily if less steeply down the valley of the Gala Water but, like the whole of the line, with many curves which were a hinderance to fast running. Galashiels was the first town of importance, followed by Melrose and St Boswells as the line undulated through the wooded valley of the Tweed to Hawick. There were several branches in the Tweed valley, one from Galashiels to Peebles, and two based on St Boswells to Duns and Tweedmouth respectively, all of which closed before the Waverley Route proper. The Tweedmouth branch, however, had its weeks of glory after the Grantshouse washouts when all the East Coast expresses were diverted that way while the main line bridges were replaced in the Eye Valley. In many ways this Tweed Valley section was scenically the most attractive of a highly scenic line. But at Hawick came another of these typical abrupt transitions with a ten mile climb to a second summit at Whitrope through countryside getting bleaker and on grades as steep as 1 in 75 in places. Again it was the curves as much as the grades that were the problem from a locomotive point of view.

Surprisingly, the Waverley Route was relatively free of major engineering features. The viaduct at Shankend and tunnel at Whitrope being the most notable exceptions. Once over the top, the line descended for ten miles through Steele Road to Newcastleton mostly at 1 in 75 round the flanks of Arnton Fell and it was not until the valley of the Liddle Water was entered at Newcastleton that the countryside became more fertile with trees to break the winds that howled off the Solway. Three miles from Whitrope was the extraordinary junction of Riccarton that could only be reached by train and was the start of another long cross country branch to Hexham built by the NB during one of its squabbles with the North Eastern. The main line crossed the Border at Kershope Foot and, apart from a short descent at 1 in 200 at Riddings, undulated from there on across the 'Debatable Lands' to Carlisle. It was a fascinating line and one that taxed its locomotives to the limit. The final years of steam I associated mostly with V2s being thrashed, though with the dieselisation of the East Coast main line some LNER Pacifics, which had been used on through passenger trains for a number of years, also turned up on Waverley Route freight trains and were thrashed accordingly. They must have found the heights of Whitrope a far cry from the Plain of York. Of all the lines between England and Scotland the Waverley Route ran through a countryside more steeped in history than any other. The Valleys of Tweed and Liddle were the scene of some of the most bitter fighting during the Border wars. Its closure was surely one of the biggest mistakes of the Beeching era leaving a vast area of South East Scotland with no rail services within forty miles and a rather poor road network into the bargain.

Above: Class 5 No 45483 pulls out of the now closed Princes Street station with an Edinburgh-Birmingham train in May 1965 not long before the station was closed and all traffic diverted to Waverley.

Top left: The effect of the closure of Princes Street station is seen in this photo of a Manchester-Edinburgh train threading through Princes Street gardens behind Nos 44925 and 44791 on 29 June 1966.

Bottom left: Class 40 No D263 in Princes Street gardens with an Aberdeen-Edinburgh express on 29 June 1966. The imposing building in the background is the Caledonian Hotel in front of Princes Street station.

Above: Smoke and spires in Princes Street gardens. The spires of the Law Courts dominate the skyline while A4 No 60019 *Bittern* does its best to obliterate them with a smoky start from Waverley on an excursion from York to Dunfermline in May 1966.

Above: A final look at the western approaches to Waverley in 1951 with a typical Glasgow-Edinburgh train hauled by B1 No 61007 *Klipspringer.*

Top right: The down 'Flying Scotsman' arrives under the cavernous roof of Waverley station in 1971 behind 'Deltic' No D9012 *Crepello.*

Bottom right: A4 No 60024 *Kingfisher* prepares to leave Waverley with an A4 Preservation Society special returning to York on 21 May 1966.

Above: The battlements of Carlton House dominate the scene at the east end of Waverley station as Class 40 No D394 prepares to leave with a Sunday evening semi-fast to Newcastle in June 1971.

Right: J36 No 65345 storms up to Blackford Hill on the old Edinburgh suburban line now used exclusively for goods traffic between Millerhill and the north and west. The train was a J36 rail-tour round the suburbs of Edinburgh on 27 August 1966 and the old ex-NB 0-6-0 designed in 1888 was still going very strongly despite some steam leaks.

Top left: Monktonhall Junction six miles east of Waverley was the most important junction between there and Berwick. It controlled the main line, a line up to Smeaton which at one time was the hub of a honeycombe of mineral lines, and also the approaches to Millerhill yard and the Edinburgh avoiding lines. In August 1951 A3 No 60042 *Singapore* passes Monktonhall box with a special train from Leeds to Aberdeen composed entirely of ex-LMS stock.

Bottom left: Also in 1951 another A3, No 60071 *Tranquil*, in its original form with circular dome approaches Monktonhall with an Edinburgh-Leeds train. 'Arthur's Seat' is prominent on the skyline.

Above: A1 No 60116 *Hal o' the Wynd* passing Monktonhall box on 7 July 1962 with a Saturday extra from Saltburn to Glasgow at a time when steam working on East Coast passenger trains was becoming rare.

Above: J38 No 65929 having dropped down the steep bank from Smeaton to the junction takes the goods lines past Monktonhall with a coal train for Millerhall Yard.

Top right: Dignity demoted, a rather grimy A4 No 60002 *Sir Murrough Wilson* approaches Monktonhall with a northbound goods on the morning of Saturday 7 July 1962. The practice of working Gateshead Pacifics north on overnight freights at summer weekends was not uncommon. The engines returned on extra passenger trains to the south later in the day.

Bottom right: The up 'Flying Scotsman' near Monktonhall in 1962 hauled by 'Deltic' No D9018 *Ballymoss.* The two-tone green livery suited the 'Deltics' far better than the overall blue which tended to make them look tubby.

Above: An up container special from Dundee to London organised by the PDL Company near Monktonhall in 1962 hauled by A3 No 60043 *Brown Jack*. These PDL trains were chartered by a shipping company and in this way anticipated the Freightliners. (Another one of them features in a footplate photo later in this volume.)

Right: Two photos at the east end of Millerhill, the first taken in August 1958, shows K3/3 Mogul No 61878 heading towards Carlisle with a goods over the Waverley Route, the earthworks for the new marshalling yard are under way. Five years later, in September 1963, B1 No 61354 seen from the same spot with an Edinburgh-Hawick train by which time the new yard was complete and in operation.

Top left: Contrast in light engines at Millerhill yard. Dignity in the form of A3 No 60092 *Fairway* and impudence in the form of Clayton No D8534.

Bottom left: Judged by any standards the Clayton Type 1s were less than successful and after a very short working life were all withdrawn. Here a line of withdrawn Class 17s wait for scrapping at Millerhill Yard with No D8565 nearest the camera and 'old Uncle Tom Cobley and all' stretching into the distance.

Above: The old North British was never known for the elegance or the comfort of its stations as shown by the pre-fab appearance of Prestonpans. Class 47 No D1577 passes southwards with a train of empty stock on 25 May 1970.

Top left: One of the very few branches in East Lothian still open for traffic is the one to North Berwick though its days would appear to be numbered. In May 1970 a two-car dmu from North Berwick to Edinburgh comes off the branch on to the main line at Drem Junction.

Bottom left: The Up 'Queen of Scots' Pullman passing Innerwick in June 1964 with 'Deltic' No D9007 *Pinza* in charge. It is here that the hard part of the southbound climb to the Penmanshiel tunnel begins.

Above: On 8 May 1965 V2 No 60975 climbs towards Granthouse with a down goods immediately after crossing the Eye Water on one of the new bridges built after the disastrous floods of 1948.

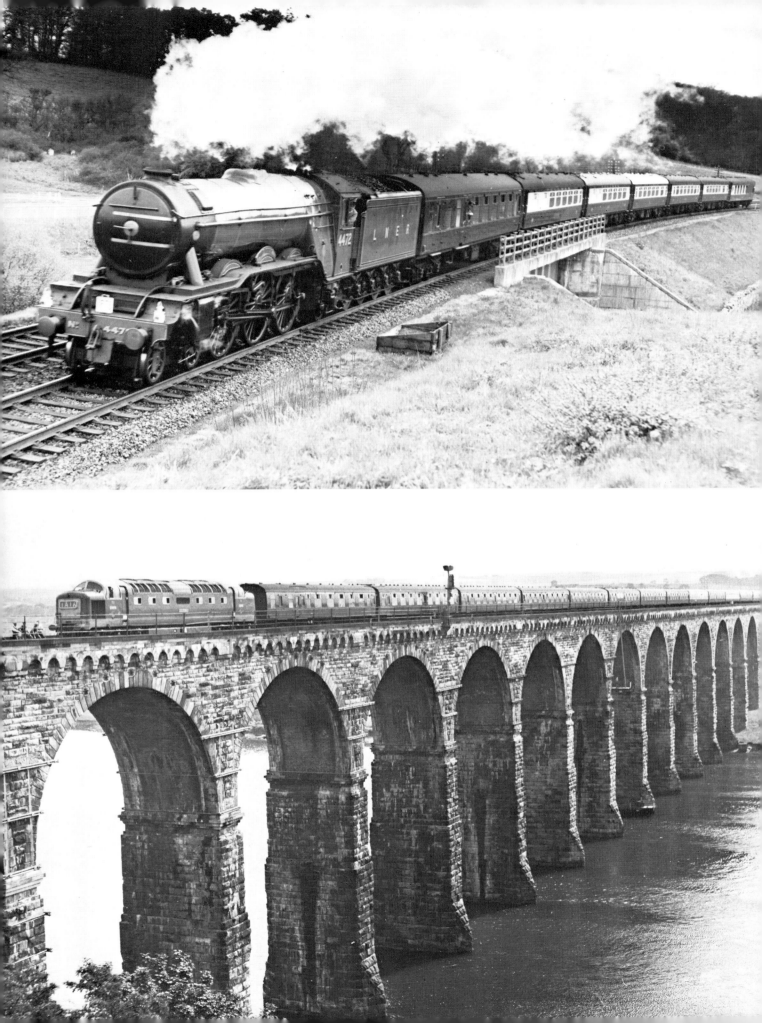

Top left: One of the first outings by No 4472 *Flying Scotsman* after her purchase and restoration by Alan Pegler. The A3 climbs towards Granthouse with 'Peglers Pullman' from Doncaster to Edinburgh, the train returning later in the day behind an A4 while *Flying Scotsman* spent a week in Scotland having her picture painted by Terence Cuneo on the Forth Bridge.

Bottom left: A London-Edinburgh express crossing the Royal Border Bridge at Berwick on Tweed on a cloudy Sunday in July 1966 hauled by 'Deltic' No D9018 *Ballymoss*.

Above: Towards the end of the Waverley Route the use of ex-LNER Pacifics became common on freight trains as on this occasion in May 1964 when A3 No 60042 *Singapore* headed south near Eskbank with a Millerhill to Kingmoor Yard goods. The gradient post indicates that the train was starting on the initial 1 in 250 stage of the long climb to Falahill.

111

Below: The northern end of the Waverley Route passed through the heart of the Lothian coalfield and A1 No 60152 passes the biggest of the pits in the area at Lady Victoria Pit box. For some time after the Waverley Route closed this pit produced enough traffic to keep a single line open from here to Millerhill but with the closure of Lady Victoria in the early 1970s even this sad rump of a magnificent line is closed and lifted.

Below: More typical power on the northern part of the Waverley Route, J37 No 64556 regains the main line after picking up a load of coal from Lady Victoria Pit. In the far background are the chimneys of a closed colliery with the delightful name Arniston Engine.

Above: Class 5 No 45254 blasts up the last mile to Falahill Summit with a Carlisle-bound goods in May 1965. Kingmoor had one or two turns over the line by this time using mainly Class 5s and the occasional 9F in contrast to Haymarket's V2s and Pacifics.

Top right: A1 No 60152 *Holyrood* breasts the last bleak yards to Falahill with a Millerhill-Kingmoor goods on 5 September 1963.

Bottom right: Once over Falahill the whole character of the line changes as it sweeps round curve after curve on the descent of the Gala Water. No D265 has charge of a southbound train of military vehicles near Fountainhall in June 1966.

Below: Fountainhall village and the Gala Water form the background to this 1965 photo of a Class 47 heading north with an excursion from Preston to Edinburgh.

Below: The morning Hawick-Edinburgh semi-fast train crosses the Gala Water amidst the rolling wooded hills near Stow hauled by B1 No 61389. While Type 2 diesels came to be used on the through trains to Carlisle, steam held sway on these Hawick trains to the bitter end.

Right: Easter Sunday finds A4 No 60031 *Golden Plover* taking water at Galashiels with an SLS excursion from Glasgow to Carlisle over the Waverley Route in 1965, the train returning to Glasgow by the Caledonian line over Beattock.

Below: Preserved A3 No 4472 *Flying Scotsman* tackling the long climb to Whitrope from the south passing through the remote Steele Road station with the Warwickshire Railway Society's 'Aberdonian' excursion in June 1965. The train was composed, rather surprisingly, of Southern Region stock.

The Central Lowlands and Fife

This area embraces much of the most heavily industrialised part of Scotland and, with the exception of parts of Fife, cannot be described as photogenic. In the few places that the railways are clear of industrial workings, the countryside is stark and bleak often scarred by old mine and quarry workings. This section is based on the lines between Edinburgh and Glasgow with their various branches and ramifications. The original Edinburgh & Glasgow line, apart from the stiff initial climb out of Queen Street, is relatively flat and featureless while the erstwhile rival Caledonian route by way of Mid-Calder and Holytown now carries little through traffic.

It was a harder proposition from a gradient point of view with long climbs to a summit at Benhar in both directions. The line from Mid-Calder to Carstairs likewise had long stretches of 1 in 100 over very cheerless windswept moorland. The third through route between Scotland's two principal cities was the ex-North British line by way of Bathgate and Coatbridge and, while still open for freight traffic, lost its passenger service soon after the war. Again this was very much an industrial line with only short lengths in open country and a gradient profile half way between the NB main line and the Caledonian route. The remaining main line in the Central Lowlands was the Caledonian line from Larbert to Motherwell forming the main link between Perth and the West Coast main line. This line again had a very heavily industrialised scenario apart from a short interlude up the wooded Cumbernauld Glen and even this has now fallen under the shadow of a new town of epic ugliness.

Between these lines there used to be a network of branches and connections mainly serving collieries and ironworks. With the general rundown of the Scottish coal and iron industry few of them survive today, indeed with hindsight many of them had as their sole justification the desire of the Caley to keep the North British out or vice versa. While Glasgow with its reputation for heavy industry would be expected to spawn many such branches, it is surprising how many there were to the south and south-east of Edinburgh, tapping the Lothians coalfield. The line from Monktonhall Junction on the East Coast main line to Smeaton tapped a web of minor mineral lines along the escarpment behind Haddington. There were also several off the Waverley Route, at either Millerhill or Hardengreen Junction, heading vaguely in the direction of Penicuik, only one of which actually got there. Apart from the Roslin branch kept alive by Bilston Glen colliery these are all now closed. One of these branches ran to Peebles by way of Leadburn. Traces of it are still visible but at the latter place another branch took off to the west heading for Heaven knows where. At the remote and tiny village of Dolphinton it met a Caledonian branch from Carstairs heading vaguely in an easterly direction. Now thereby hangs a tale. Each company had its own station at Dolphinton, giving the village as many stations as it had shops, one station on each side of the main road from Edinburgh to Moffat with a link between them. I mention this to show how old emnities die hard in this part of Scotland for, during World War 2, there was a big Army camp at Dunsyre near Dolphinton and to this establishment one fine day the LMS ran a troop train of twelve vehicles hauled, if my informant can be believed, by a 'Greyback' (Caley Class 60 4-6-0). (As my informant was the driver this is probably correct.)

Now the general idea was that this train, having disgorged the soldiery, should run empty stock to Dolphinton (Caledonian), the loco run round and return tender first to Carstairs, but alas, the loop at Dolphinton would take only six coaches. However after some thought the stationmaster at Dolphinton (Caledonian) decided that six coaches should be left in his loop, the loco should proceed under the road bridge and round the remaining six at Dolphinton (NB) before rejoining the train at Cisalpine Dolphinton, as Caesar would have said

Right: At one time the area immediately south-east of Edinburgh was a mass of short branch lines mostly in connection with coal mines. One such was the Roslin branch and on 16 October 1965 the preserved GNSR 4-4-0 No 49 *Gordon Highlander* is seen approaching the terminus with a Branch Line Society excursion embracing several of the lesser-known lines round Edinburgh. This was to be her last public appearance.

but oh no! The stationmaster at the NB end of the arrangement would have nothing to do with it until he had explicit permission from Waverley, to let a train of the rival company into his station — and — this at the height of the war! After the antics of the battle of Dolphinton it is a relief to turn to the LNER main line from Glasgow to Edinburgh, a line, since the closure of Buchanan Street, that must be about the busiest in the country between Cowlairs and Greenhill Upper Junction near Falkirk. Not only has passenger traffic increased on this line but the vast petrochemical complex and docks at Grangemouth has given bulk freight traffic a tremendous boost so that even with modern signalling parts of it are now just about at saturation point. Its main points of engineering interest are the two great viaducts near Bathgate Junction and west of Linlithgow. Its niche in railway history is a sad one as it has had probably more serious accidents per mile than any in the country.

Turning now to Fife. This was North British territory but again honeycombed with branches almost entirely connected with what was once a very extensive mining industry. Two main lines ran across Fife. One ran from the Forth Bridge to Dundee and the other was the Glenfarg Route to Perth. The latter is now closed and Perth traffic follows the main line to Ladybank Junction and then cuts across by way of Newburgh to Bridge of Earn which was the original route before the opening of the Forth Bridge. There was also a very scenic line round the coast from Leuchars to Thornton by way of St Andrews and a beautiful single line that wandered down the Devon Valley from Kinross to Alloa. In addition there is a line from Stirling to Dunfermline through Alloa with a coastal branch by way of Kincardie which, on account of two major power stations at Kincardine and Longannet, is now the more important of the two. Some of this branch line building can also be ascribed to fear of the Caledonian which cast eyes at Fife from both Stirling and Dundee and did in fact get as near as Alloa with a branch from Larbert. It only needed some enterprising group of citizens to start a branch, run out of cash and mutter 'we'll go and see the Caley in case they want it' for the North British to step in smartly and complete the line. Rumour has it that the sonorously named East of Fife Central railway was built by this means, though from the start it was goods only and only got a passenger service over the last mile at Lochty when John Cameron bought the Gresley Pacific *Union of South Africa*. Surely this is the only case in Britain where a goods only branch got a passenger service at a time when most passenger carrying branches were losing theirs.

Below: Another branch near Edinburgh now closed was the Kirkliston branch which left the Edinburgh-Glasgow main line at Kirkliston Junction and worked its way across country to join the main line to Fife at Dalmeny Junction. The Scottish Region's preserved ex-North British 4-4-0 No 256 *Glen Douglas* leaves the long-closed Kirkliston station on 13 April 1963 with an SLS special taking a devious route to Fife.

Below: Apart from the North British main line and the old Caledonian line through Shotts there was a third route from Glasgow to Edinburgh by way of Airdrie and Bathgate. This line lost its passenger trains shortly after the war and scenically was a disaster. Its only photogenic feature was the reservoir of Caldercruix seen here behind an RCTS excursion hauled by ex-NB 4-4-0 *Glen Douglas* in 1965, in action for the last time.

Above: Of the three routes between Glasgow and Edinburgh the Caledonian was the most difficult from a gradient point of view, starting with the long climb out of Edinburgh to Midcalder Junction where the lines to Carstairs and Glasgow separated. In May 1964 an International Conference on Large Dams (I am *not* making this up!) was held in Edinburgh and to help their deliberations the delegates were taken for a cruise on the Clyde. One of the two special trains run is seen here near Currie on the outskirts of Edinburgh en route for Gourock behind Class 5s Nos 45483 and 45389.

Above: The Caley route from Glasgow to Edinburgh features again in this picture of two Claytons Nos D8526 and D8520 passing Hartwood station with an Orangemen's special from Glasgow to Shotts.

Left: From Midcalder Junction the line to Carstairs climbed to an altitude of over 800ft at Cobbinshaw before dropping down into the Clyde Valley. GNSR No 49 pauses for a photo stop at Auchengray with a Branch Line Society special on 16 October 1965.

Bottom left: Like all the stations between Midcalder and Carstairs the very attractive one at Carnwath is now closed and demolished. Caley 0-4-4T No 55124 passes Carnwath with an enthusiasts' excursion from Edinburgh to Broughton on 30 September 1961.

Above: 'Austerity' tackles the Cumbernauld Bank some 12 miles east of Glasgow with an oil train from Grangemouth to the south. The loco is No 90560 and is assisted in the rear by J37 No 64537. This area has changed out of all recognition since this picture was taken in 1963. It is now covered by a 'New Town' of more than usual architectural hideousness.

Top left: Class 27 No D5399 heads one of the Edinburgh-Glasgow pull and push trains into Falkirk High station on 2 November 1971 after a dismal day of rain. The rear loco of the combination was No D5403.

Bottom left: Cadder Yard is the main marshalling yard for traffic to the east and north of Glasgow situated on the Glasgow-Edinburgh main line some eight miles east of Queen Street. On 14 May 1971 one of the recently introduced pull and push trains passes Cadder box en route to Edinburgh with Class 27 No D5410 leading and No D5407 trailing.

Above: Two months before the total withdrawal of the Class, North British-built Class 29 No D6132 moves out of Grangemouth docks with a brake-van in tow.

Above: Class 37s No D6857 and D6843 approach Cadder from the east with a Grangemouth-Braehead power station oil train. Oil trains from Grangemouth are the heaviest trains on the very intensively-used section between Falkirk and Cowlairs.

Above: Towed by Clayton No D8575 the preserved 'Shire' class 4-4-0 No 246 *Morayshire* approaches Dalmeny Junction on 16 June 1966 while being moved from store at ICI sidings at Ardeer to the Navy's Queen Elizabeth Yard near Dalmeny. At the time *Morayshire* was considered to be beyond steaming again, but nine years later was fit enough to take her place in the Shildon Cavalcade.

Above: V2 No 60816 on an up PDL container special meets an unidentified Class 40 with a northbound parcels train in the woods at Kinghorn, 25 May 1964.

Top right: Fireman's view of the Forth Bridge climbing through North Queensferry station on a dull May day in 1964. The loco was V2 No 60816 and the train a Dundee-London PDL container special.

Bottom right: Positively the last steam loco to work in Scotland apart from industrial and preserved engines, J36 No 65345 an NB 0-6-0 of 1888 vintage happily shunts at Seafield Colliery (Fife) on 23 March 1967; three months *after* all BR steam in Scotland was officially withdrawn!

Left: Class J37 No 64569 duly polished up for the occasion working the RCTS Fife Coast Excursion between Dundee and Thornton Junction. These ex-NB 0-6-0s known locally as the 'S' class were very popular in Fife. The first photo is taken crossing a tidal inlet at Guard Bridge and the second exchanging tablets at Crail.

Above: B1 No 61245 crossing the viaduct at Markinch with a northbound train of empty wagons on a frosty November morning in 1965.

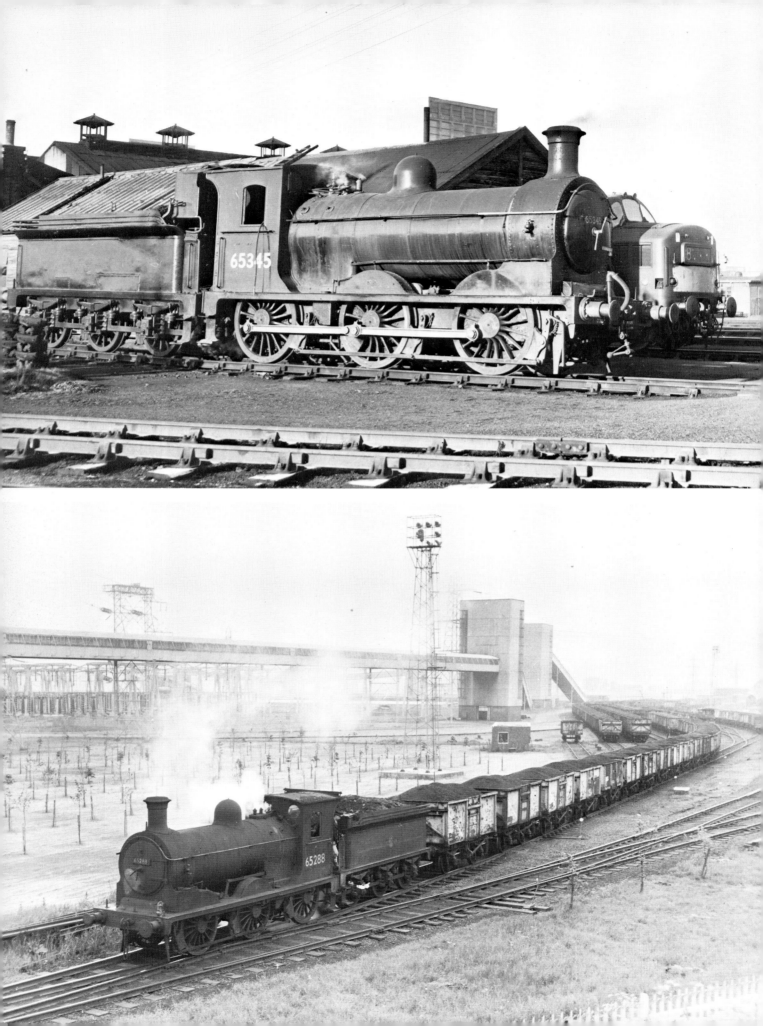

Top left: Two styles of fronts at Thornton Junction shed. J36 No 65345, known as 'Dr Findlay's engine' as it was used in the TV series in a scene taken at Caldwell on the Barrhead-Kilmarnock Joint line, of all places. The nose of a Class 37 is in the background.

Bottom left: One might be forgiven for thinking that the J36 class were indestructible for 65288 having worked in from Manor Powis spent much of the day in June 1966 shunting the extensive yards at Kincardine power station despite a mildly burned smokebox door.

Above: B1 No 61072 pilots 'Austerity' 2-8-0 No 90041 down the steep single line from Kincardine Junction with a load of coal from Alloa sidings to Kincardine Power Station on 11 June 1966.

Right: 'Austerity' 2-8-0 No 90465 at Lumphinnans Junction on a snowy evening in November 1965 with the breakdown train returning to Thornton Junction from Alloa.

Below: Lumphinnans Junction again with a coal train headed towards Thornton through a snowy landscape on 22 November 1965.

Stirling to Perth and the North East

My reasons for treating this as a separate section are twofold. First geographically it is the transition between the Lowlands and Highlands, and, second, it is the trunk from which all but one of the lines to the far north of Scotland spring. In many respects Perth is to Central Scotland what Carlisle is to Cumbria and South Scotland, a meeting place for several very important lines dictated by its geographical position as the lowest convenient crossing of the River Tay. From the south the main line was that of the Caledonian from Glasgow and the Clyde Valley by way of Stirling. In addition the North British line from Edinburgh joined this route at Hilton Junction on the southern outskirts. Though the main line over Glenfarg is now closed there is still a link by way of Ladybank and Newburgh which, despite being single, carries a lot of traffic though some has been diverted by way of Larbert and Falkirk which was the main route prior to the opening of the Forth Bridge. To the north the Caledonian main line continued through Forfar and Kinnaber Junction to Aberdeen. It is joined at the latter by the NB line from Edinburgh by way of Dundee and the Forth and Tay bridges. Eight miles north of Perth the Highland line to Inverness left the Caledonian line at Stanley Junction while a line to Dundee veered sharply to the east in Perth station, crossed the Tay on a single track bridge before once again becoming double track to Dundee. Since Beeching the pattern has altered slightly insofar as the Caledonian line now runs as a single track branch from Stanley Junction to Forfar at one end and another single track branch from Kinnaber to Brechin at the other. All through traffic from Glasgow to Aberdeen takes the slower more circuitous route by Dundee. With the increase of traffic to and from Aberdeen there have been rumours lately that this direct line may be restored but I feel that by the time anyone has made a decision the North Sea oil that has made Aberdeen so busy may have run dry.

Returning to Stirling, the main line has a short level start across the Forth, paralleled to the east by the old North British line to Alloa. From a mile south of Bridge of Allan it starts the six mile climb to Kinbuck on gradients of 1 in 100 steepening over the last two miles to 1 in 88. This is a severe test of locomotive performance especially over the initial three miles from Bridge of Allan in autumn and winter where the line winds up the beautiful wooded valley of the Allan Water to Dunblane but which is very prone to fallen leaves in the autumn and pockets of frost in winter. Dunblane was the junction of the Caley route to Oban that was earmarked for closure even before a severe rock fall in Glen Ogle caused its premature demise. Oban trains then had to be diverted by the West Highland line and Crianlarich. For a few years this lingered on as a branch as far as Callander but in the late 1960s this too was closed and lifted which in view of the increasing tourist traffic to the area and vast forestry developments seems to have been a mistake. Beyond Dunblane, while still following the Allan Water, the main line runs through more open country and some of the richest farming land in Scotland. Once over Kinbuck the line is level for two miles then rises again through Blackford on easy grades to the summit at Gleneagles. This was the junction for a branch to Crieff which at one time went on to Comrie and then followed the north side of Loch Earn to Balquidder on the Oban line. I never knew the branch operating beyond Crieff but the Loch Earn stretch must have been superbly beautiful.

Beyond Gleneagles the line drops for nearly three miles at 1 in 100 into the valley of the River Earn where the gradients ease finishing up with a couple of level miles to Hilton Junction and Perth. The Perth-Dundee line, following the north bank of the Tay, is virtually level throughout and was the last stamping ground of the famous Caledonian Single before its withdrawal from regular service. The line to the north climbs gradually to Stanley Junction and

then has long straight and level stretches
to Forfar and beyond which was
considered in both Caledonian and LMS
days to be the racing ground of Scotland.
Beyond Kinnaber the line climbs on
broken grades to Drumlithie Summit
then drops steeply to Stonehaven before
undulating along the coast to Cove Bay
with some short sharp gradients as steep
as 1 in 100. From Cove Bay the line
drops steeply for the last five miles to
Aberdeen. Again this area is rich in
viaducts especially round Montrose and
from Stonehaven to Cove Bay where it
runs along an escarpment high above the
North Sea that is bisected by streams
flowing in deep valleys.

The North East was very much Great
North of Scotland territory with a
surprising number of lines considering
the relative sparseness of the population.
Here again the Great North had a
constant fear of the Highland breathing
down its neck and so went in for some
pretty competitive railway building to
keep the Highlanders out. I have to
confess that the North East is neglected
in this book as I very seldom had cause
to be in these parts and by the time I
came back to live in Scotland they were
mainly diesel-operated anyhow.
Generally speaking the Great North was
an easy terrain to master apart from the
branch up the Dee Valley to Ballater and
the meandering line up the Spey Valley
between Craigellachie and Boat of
Garten, this at one time being intended
as a counter attack on Inverness to keep
the Highland in its place. It so frightened
the latter that it spent a great deal of
money it could ill afford building the
direct line from Aviemore to Inverness
over Slochd and while this effectively
kept the Great North out of Inverness
there were many empty sporrans in the
Highland capital for some years after.
The history of Scottish Railways is one of
feuding on a degree never envisaged
even by the most blood-thirsty of the
Clans. The Highland and the Great North
were bitter enemies, the North British
and the Caledonian were very wary of
each other and the latter fought with
everyone in sight, especially the Glasgow
& South Western. The long running
emnity between these two made the
London, Chatham & Dover and the
South Eastern look like a honeymoon
couple. I wish I had known the Great
North in steam days as it had some very
attractive routes notably the coast line
from Elgin to Cairnie Junction near
Huntly. Alas, there is little left of it now
apart from the main line from Aberdeen
to Keith and the line to Fraserburgh, now
goods only; even the branch from Maud
to Peterhead has gone, though had the
North Sea oil boom started a couple of
years sooner this might well have been
saved.

Below: The steepest part of the climb between Stirling and Perth is up through the wooded glen of the Allan Water. On 2 March 1963, with vestiges of snow still lying about the tracks, Class 5 No 45049 makes a rousing attack on this bank with a Carlisle-Perth goods.

Below: Standard Class 2 Mogul No 78053 drops down the glen of the Allan Water between Bridge of Allan and Dunblane with a pick-up goods from Callender to Stirling on 2 March 1963.

Top left: A4 No 60027 *Merlin* with a Dundee-Glasgow express between Dunblane and Bridge of Allan in June 1965.

Bottom left: No 46236 *City of Bradford* leaves the short Dunblane tunnel and crosses the Allan Water with the midday Perth-Euston express on 2 March 1963.

Above: The morning Crewe-Perth semi-fast train approaching Dunblane from the south on 11 August 1964, hauled by 'Clan' No 72009 *Clan Stewart*.

Above: The 1.30pm Aberdeen-Glasgow train leaving Dunblane station on 27 August 1965 behind A4 No 60009 *Union of South Africa.* This engine has now been preserved by John Cameron at Lochty and is used to power enthusiasts' specials on some of the Scottish Region lines.

Top right: V2 No 60973 leaving Dunblane with a Glasgow-Aberdeen train in March 1963 with the Caledonian Oban line diverging in the foreground.

Bottom right: An up express from Aberdeen to Glasgow in charge of V2 No 60970 leaving Gleneagles station on 21 September 1963. Though within yards of the summit of the Perth-Stirling stretch this southbound start from Gleneagles was a difficult one, especially in poor weather conditions.

Above: By September 1963 the local
services on the Gleneagles-Crieff Branch
were in the hands of a diesel railbus. On the
21st of the month the railbus, not unusually,
had broken down and a steam service was
substituted. Class 5 No 44722 works a two
coach train from Crieff to Gleneagles near
Tillibardine Halt.

Top right: Preserved NB 4-4-0 No 256 *Glen
Douglas* heads for Perth at Bridge of Earn
after working an RCTS special from Thornton
Junction by way of Ladybank on 28 August
1965.

Bottom right: Hilton Junction two miles
south of Perth was the meeting place of the
Caledonian line from Stirling and the NB line
across Fife. Standard Class 5 No 73006
comes off the former with a Glasgow-
Inverness train in October 1965.

Above: One of the joys of train photography is the unexpected. What could be more unexpected than the sight of 'Duchess' No 46255 *City of Hereford* passing through the mists of the Earn Valley at Hilton Junction with a special train of steel girders from Motherwell to Perth. Seen from the signal box on 21 September 1963.

Top right: The down 'Granite City' express from Glasgow to Aberdeen approaching Perth station on 8 September 1962 with two NBL Class 29 diesels in charge, Nos D6120 and D6105. At the time I was not amused, hoping for one of the ex-LNER Pacifics recently transferred to St Rollox for these jobs, but in retrospect LNER Pacifics lasted far longer than NBLs.

Bottom right: Class 47 No D1968 heads an Aberdeen-Edinburgh express across the graceful stone viaduct at the south entrance to the Montrose basin on 5 August 1972. This viaduct is situated on the single line section between Montrose and Usan box some 1½ miles to the south.

Right: On 5 September 1970 the Great North of Scotland Railway Association ran the Peterhead Farewell Excursion on the day the branch officially closed to passengers. Hauled by Class 26 No D5307 the train pauses at Ellon on its return journey to Aberdeen.

Below: Aberdeen station in the late summer of 1951 with Standard 4MTT No 80028 waiting in one of the bay platforms at the north end with a train for Fraserburgh when there was still a passenger service on the Buchan Lines.

The Highlands

In this section I am covering four routes to the Highland areas of Scotland: The Highland main line; the Far North & Kyle lines; the West Highland line, and the Oban line. Much to my regret, I am forced into doing this for two reasons. First, lack of space and second, lack of suitable material as by the time I had come to know most of these lines well, diesels had taken over. While in steam days it was a case of Class 5s with everything, my photographic records tend to be Class 27s with everything and undoubtedly, though we may not have appreciated it at the time, the former was a far more interesting diet. One thing that has to be understood in any consideration of the railays of the Highlands is that while most railways in Britain were built to link existing centres of population and trade, these lines were built to open up the country in an effort to reverse the notorious Highland clearances and bring people back. The one exception to this is the Highland main line from Inverness to Perth which was built specifically to link Inverness with the south. In many ways, although it may not be the most spectacular of the lines under review, it is the most remarkable; indeed probably the most remarkable in Britain for it is in every sense a main line well laid out. Inevitably there are long gradients but without the sharp ups and downs of its bretheren. Far from lacking in curves these, generally speaking, are of fairly large radius. This broad concept, and the fact that it was built in three years, is a tremendous tribute to Joseph Mitchell its Inverness-born engineer who inherited the Locke and Grainger ability to use landforms to the utmost advantage with the minimum of heavy earthworks. Indeed, the hardest length of the Highland both from a locomotive and an engineering point of view was the Slochd cut-off from Aviemore to Inverness built long after Mitchell's original line over Dava Moor from Forres.

From the junction with the Caledonian at Stanley, the first section as far as Pitlochry has some short sharp grades notably on either side of Kingswood Crossing. It abounds in curves but this length was not originally laid out by Mitchell. From Pitlochry to Blair Atholl is an undulating climb through the Pass of Killicrankie but it is at Blair that the hard work really begins with the 18-mile climb to Drumochter Summit much of it at 1 in 70 on open hillsides exposed to every blizzard that blows. This section from Blair Atholl to Dalwhinnie was double track but BR played the Grand Old Duke of York, first having singled it to the top of the hill ten years ago, now laying the second track down again to accommodate an upsurge of traffic. From the summit there is a long descent to Newtonmore on broken gradients the steepest of which is 1 in 80. This is followed by an easy undulating length to Aviemore where the original line climbed again over Dava Moor before joining the Inverness-Keith line at Forres. The new line by Carrbridge to Slochd Summit is far the hardest part of the route with long climbs at 1 in 60 both sides of the summit and the two great viaducts at Tomatin and Culloden into the bargain.

The ramifications of the Highland north of Inverness were very much lines built to open up the country and to do so as cheaply as possible. The Far North Line is a particularly good example of this with its lengthy detours to Lairg and up the Helmsdale to Forsinard where following the coastal route might well have been easier to build apart from some viaducts across the estuaries. Certainly by going up through Forsinard the line was able to throw off a branch to Thurso at Georgemas Junction which is now more important than the line to Wick, but the snow-swept heights of Forsinard and the improbably named Fairy Hillocks were a stiff price to pay.

The other line still surviving north of Inverness is the old Dingwall and Skye line leaving the Far North line at Dingwall and running westwards to Strome Ferry on Loch Carron and which was later extended to Kyle of Lochalsh. This line though not as difficult as some of the Highlands railways has one prodigious climb from Fodderty Junction to Raven Rock Summit. Nearly four miles at 1 in 50, it is the steepest passenger carrying line in the country apart from the Cowlairs Incline out of Glasgow Queen Street. The sad part about the Raven Rock climb is that it was wholly unnecessary as there was a far easier route through Strathpeffer that was blocked by an uncooperative landowner, the only case of its kind in the whole annals of the Highland Railway. Undoubtedly the finest part of the Kyle line lies in the last miles from Strathcarron along the shores of Loch Carron. It has only become accessible in the last few years with the building of a road paralleling the line from Strome Ferry. Like the Dingwall and Skye line, the Oban line was built to reach a port on the west coast with shipping contacts to the Islands of the Hebrides. Though started as a private venture it was soon absorbed by the Caledonian whose line it branched off at Dunblane to run by way of Callender and up the steep Glen Ogle for 4½ miles at 1 in 60. Once over the summit it dropped equally steeply to Luib before undulating to Crianlarich, throwing off on its way a branch down to Killin on Loch Tay. This section is now closed and the Oban trains rejoin the old Caledonian route at Crianlarich before tackling a climb through Tyndrum to another summit of 840ft. Thereafter a steep drop to Dalmally is followed by a generally undulating length to Connel Bridge, including the spectacular Pass of Brander with its avalanche warning signals. At Connel Bridge there was a branch for Ballachulish while the main line climbed steeply to a last summit at Glencruitten before dropping down 2½ miles at 1 in 50 to Oban which has one of the most attractive stations in Scotland, alongside the water's edge.

The West Highland, again built privately, but very much in the pocket of the North British had grandiose ideas of getting to Inverness. Mercifully it didn't as if it had, Inverness would probably have had no railways at all by now. However the prospect of an outlet to the Western sea was too tempting and the line finally bore westwards to Fort William with a highly spectacular extension built on to Mallaig some years later. Both the Mallaig extension and the Kyle line have been under threat of closure since the war and logically there is only room for one 'road to the Isles'. In the end it will probably be the Kyle line, as the fish traffic from Mallaig is diminishing fast while traffic to Kyle is on the increase. The West Highland is a line of long steep gradients culminating in a summit of 1,315ft at Currour on the northern edge of Rannoch Moor but unlike the Highland, it is a line of intense curvature. Even on the easier stretches many short sharp changes of grade rule out any chances of fast running quite apart from the fact that the ruling grade is 1 in 55 against the Highland's 1 in 60. It is a line of breathtaking views first on the long climb above Loch Long to Glen Douglas, then along the west side of Loch Lomond and up Glen Falloch followed by more climbing to Tyndrum, a short drop round the Horseshoe bend to Bridge of Orchy. It then runs across the glacial wastes of Rannoch Moor before dropping on an inclined plane down Loch Treig and through the Monessie Gorge to Fort William, it is a line that cannot be described but has to be travelled over on a fine spring day to be appreciated. Luckily, on account of the paper pulp mills and aluminium industry at Fort William, its future at the time of writing seems reasonably secure.

The Highland Railway South of Inverness

Above: Though the Highland Railways exercised running powers over the Caledonian from Perth, the start of its own metals was at Stanley Junction some 8 miles to the north. Class 26s D5334 and D5327 swing on to the Highland line with an Glasgow-Inverness train on 18 September 1973 while Class 47 No 1566 waits on what used to be the Caley's main line to Aberdeen with the daily goods from Forfar.

Left: Stranger on the Highland line at Pitlochry on 15 April 1969 when 'Deltic' No D9019 *Royal Highland Fusilier* pilots Class 26 D5338 on the Perth-Inverness mail. The 'Deltic' was working to Inverness to take a special to the Army football final at Aldershot that evening where the regiment it was named after was competing.

Above: During the last week of August 1965, the Centenary of the Highland Railway was marked by a stroke of genius on the part of the Scottish Region. All week the preserved Jones Goods 4-6-0 worked a series of two return trips per day between Inverness and Forres hauling preserved Caledonian coaches. This photo shows the ensemble at Blair Atholl on Saturday 30 August returning to Glasgow.

Left: Crossings at Newtonmore. With snow still on the hills in April 1969 No D5328 and an unidentified Class 24 approach with the morning Glasgow-Inverness train while two Class 26s wait with the mid-morning Inverness-Glasgow. Three and a half years later, the evening Inverness-Glasgow train with Nos D5331 and D5330 in charge wait while sister engines Nos D5335 and D5339, approach with an afternoon train from Edinburgh. Newtonmore was the changeover point for the Inverness and Perth crews on these services.

Above: Crossing the Spey on a typical Highland viaduct No D5315 heads a special train from Invergordon to Glasgow in connection with a National Trust cruise that arrived at Invergordon early in the day 18 August 1973.

Top left: Ex-Highland 4-6-0 No 103 with the two preserved Caledonian coaches returning to Glasgow on 30 August 1965 after working the Highland Centenary trips to and from Forres during the week. Framed by trees and with Loch Insh in the background the train is about a mile south of Kincraig.

Bottom left: An Inverness-Edinburgh train climbs away from Millburn Junction with the Black Isle in the background. The loco is Class 5 No 45478 and the short train indicates that it was picking up a portion at Aviemore that had run by Forres, a practice common in 1950. The fourth vehicle is one of the ex-Pullman Cars used on the Highland for a few years after the war.

Right and below: Two photos taken within an hour on the shores of the Beauly Firth in 1951 showing contrasting generations of locomotives. Standard 5 No 73005 newly-built heads an Inverness-Aberdeen train near Allanfearn while Caley 4-4-0 No 54487 passes the same spot with a train from Aberdeen.

The Highland Railway North of Inverness

Top left: Crossing the Ness viaduct in Inverness a train of empty grain hoppers in connection with the distillery traffic is hauled by Class 40 No D363 in September 1973. These Company trains were known locally as 'the Whisky trains' and this particular one is en route from Invergordon to Doncaster.

Bottom left: Crossing the Caledonian Canal at Clachnaharry a northbound goods probably for Invergordon is unexpectedly hauled by ex-Caledonian 4-4-0 No 54472 in 1950.

Above: The evening Inverness-Wick and Thurso train on the outskirts of Inverness in the summer of 1950 hauled by Class 5s Nos 45457 and 45491.

Top left: The only double track stretch of the Far North line was some six miles between Clachnaharry & Clunes which, while now singled, may be doubled again with the growth of traffic from Invergordon. Class 5s near Lentran with a Wick-Inverness train in 1951, No 44799 in the lead. The second last vehicle is a restaurant car transferred from the corresponding northbound train at the Mound.

Bottom left: Class 24 No D5113 at Dingwall with a Wick-Inverness goods on 20 September 1973. The station architecture of Dingwall is unusual for the Highland being very ornate, presumably on account of its proximity to the once popular spa resort of Strathpeffer.

Above: Georgemas Junction the most northerly in Britain in September 1973 with Class 26 No D5341 approaching from Thurso while Class 24 No D5116 waits in the foreground with the Wick-Inverness portion of the mid-morning train from the Far North. In recent years Thurso has become the more important railhead of the two and the Wick portions are normally only two coaches.

165

Below: The end of the line. Class 24 No D5116 prepares to leave for Inverness with the midday train on 19 September 1973. Despite their rough riding, the Class 24s were liked in Inverness being reputedly stronger on the hills than the 26s. The signal box and signals at Wick are now demolished.

Below: The first station of importance on the Kyle line that branches westwards at Dingwall, is Garve which is the railhead for Ullapool. The connecting bus loads mail in the station yard off the 10.40am Inverness-Kyle train hauled by the inevitable Class 26 on a damp day in 1968.

Above: One of the very last mixed trains in Britain. The Mondays, Fridays and Saturdays only 7.05am from Dingwall to Kyle near Attadale Platform, hauled by D5341 in the autumn of 1973.

Above: The morning goods from Inverness to Kyle approaching Plockton, dwarfed by high cliffs and hemmed in by Loch Carron. In 1968 this train was regularly hauled by two diesels, in this case Class 26s Nos D5334 and D5340, partly on account of the weight of the train and partly to balance engine workings.

The Oban Line

Above: The SLS Special of Good Friday 1963 ran from Glasgow to Crianlarich by way of Callander and returned over the West Highland. Composed of the Caledonian Single No 123 and the two preserved Caley coaches it also ran from brilliant sun through blinding snow showers and made a trip down the branch to Killin in passing. Standard 2-6-4T No 80093 waits at the terminus ready to return to Killin Junction in a mixture of sunshine and snowflakes.

Top right: During one of the sunny periods the Special passes Luib station behind No 123 with freshly fallen snow all round.

Bottom right: The Caley Single at Crianlarich Lower Junction in a blinding snow shower which obscures the West Highland viaduct normally visible in the background. The train is coming off the Caledonian line on to the spur linking it with the West Highland at Crianlarich Upper station before propelling to the latter and turning for the return to Glasgow.

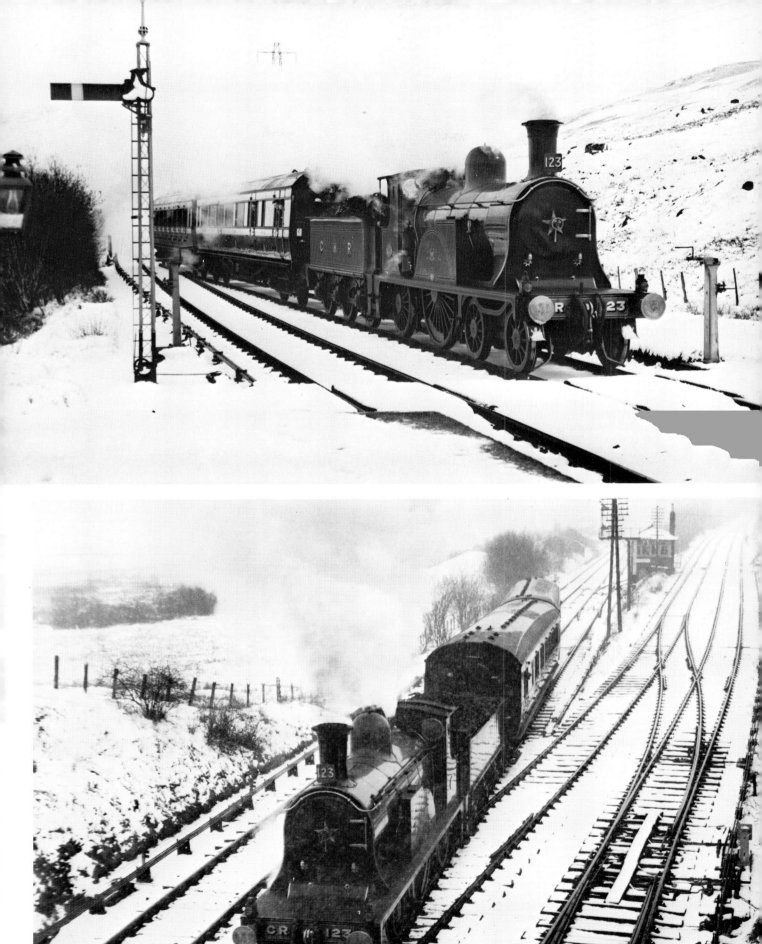

Top left: Oban station has a somewhat deserted air as NBL Class 29 No D6101 waits to leave with a train for Glasgow in 1968 at a time when these engines were in regular use. Their good riding qualities on the twisty West Highland and Oban routes were appreciated by the crews even if their unreliability was not.

The West Highland Line

Bottom left: The West Highland line proper starts from Craigendoran Junction on the North British Helensburgh line, now electrified. A Class 27 comes off the West Highland with the early Oban-Glasgow service at Craigendoran seen from the cab of sister engine D5367 working the 10.05 Glasgow-Mallaig on 5 September 1972.

Above: An Oban-Glasgow train on West Highland metals. The 12.25 Oban-Glasgow at the head of Glen Falloch, south of Crianlarich, hauled by NBL Class 29 No D6112 in 1968. In the background are some remnants of the old Caledonian Forest.

Right: There would appear to be no trouble with the train heating boiler of Class 27 No D5351 as it waits in Bridge of Orchy station on 5 March 1971 though some of the steam heating hoses would appear in need of attention! The train is the afternoon Fort William to Glasgow conveying through sleeping cars to Kings Cross (5th and 6th vehicles).

Below: The morning Fort William-Glasgow train at Crianlarich Upper station in March 1971 hauled by Class 27 No D5361. With the closure of the Caley line from Dunblane, the diversion of the Oban traffic to the West Highland, and the increase in timber and paper pulp traffic from Corpach, Crianlarich is now a busier junction than at any time in its life.

Ayrshire and Galloway

This final section covers what was possibly the most varied railway working in Scotland, ranging from two long heavily graded single lines conveying heavy boat trains at one end of the spectrum and short locals at the other. In addition, as far as Ayr and to a lesser extent Girvan, there is an extensive if dilatory commuter service from Glasgow and, in the middle so to speak, the once heavy and still sizeable mineral traffic in the Ayrshire coalfields. The southern limb of these lines was the so-called 'Port Road' from Dumfries to Stranraer though this was built in two parts, the line from Dumfries to Castle Douglas was pure Glasgow & South Western. The continuation to Stranraer was originally the Portpatrick & Wigtownshire railway that took great care to avoid all centres of population between Castle Douglas and Newton Stewart by wandering up Loch Ken and then across the wild moors of inland Galloway. To be sure, it catered for Gatehouse of Fleet and New Galloway with stations seven and three miles from their respective towns! The PP&W was always in trouble, mainly through its own making, by being stupid enough to think it could play off the arch enemies, the Caledonian and G&SW against one another at profit to itself. This did not work and in the end the line became the most joint in Britain being owned in parts by the LNW, the Midland, the Caledonian, and the G&SW though the latter two companies were left to work it. The original goal was Portpatrick where the government of the day, as is the wont of governments, decided to build a packet station for the Irish traffic in a totally unsuitable location. The Stranraer Harbour branch was an after-thought but to-day is the main port for Northern Ireland and the Portpatrick line is closed beyond Stranraer. Closed also is the entire line from Dumfries to Challoch Junction near Dunragit with all traffic now reaching Stranraer by way of Ayr and Girvan. Before leaving the 'Port Road', however, mention must be made of its one and only branch to Whithorn with a short spur to Garlieston. Even in its last years (it closed in October 1964 nine months before the PP&W) it was a line of tremendous charm and character having more than a whiff of Irish country branches about it both in its landscape and its easy-going ways. In PP&W days this line was joint between the Caley and G&SW, the big boys from the south quite wisely having nothing to do with it. At one time it was worked alternately, three years by each company with the result that nobody bothered to maintain it and how there was never a bad accident down there I will never know ... if there had been it would undoubtedly have been blamed on the Fairies.

The surviving line from Girvan to Stranraer was also a child of sorrow. It was built as the Girvan & Portpatrick Junction Railway, no doubt on the assumption that once open the G&SW would buy it up at a goodly profit. This was not to be and it was left to struggle on for a few years on secondhand stock mostly from, of all unlikely places, the North London Railway. This may well have given rise to the theory in LMS days, and still held today, that all SW Scotland gets in the way of engines are 'The Lunnon Midland Region's haund me doons'. The Girvan-Stranraer line is nothing if not dramatic, starting with four miles off the platform end at 1 in 54 up to the Pinmore tunnel then a steep descent down the Stinchar Valley to Pinwherry including the superb curved Pinmore Viaduct probably the loveliest of all the G&SW viaducts. From Pinwherry there is the long climb of eight miles through Barrhill to the Chirmorie Summit followed by a descent to Glenwhilly mostly at 1 in 100, a short rise and three miles at 1 in 57 down the dreaded Swan's Neck to New Luce, thereafter the going is relatively easy to Stranraer.

One feature of the Barrhill/New Luce length is its incredible bleakness, rivalling Rannoch Moor or Forsinard, mile after mile of high, exposed peat bogs that are featureless and utterly black on a winter's night. While snow is relatively uncommon in this part of Scotland both routes to Stranraer have had their share of trouble with trains trapped for days by blizzards. Even as recently as 1965 passengers had to be rescued from a train trapped at Barrhill by helicopter.

The next stage from Girvan to Maybole is also steep in places and with very broken gradients. It is also the most scenic of the whole line, running up the wooded Girvan Valley containing what must be the most rural colliery (now closed) at Bargany. From Maybole to Ayr the line continues as a switchback but through more open arable country. Three miles south of Ayr, at Dalrymple Junction, the Dalmellington branch joins from the south which, while now closed between Waterside & Dalmellington, still carries a heavy coal traffic from the former. An interesting conjecture concerning this line is that at one time there were thoughts of continuing it beyond Dalmellington towards New Galloway which could have been one of the reasons for the 'Port Road's' apparently aimless wanderings round Loch Ken. The main line from Ayr to Glasgow, one of the earliest in Scotland, is flat and lacking in any noteworthy features but carries a heavy commuter traffic. Ayr is now the main concentration point for the coal traffic from the remaining pits in the area, some of which is shipped from Ayr Harbour and some re-marshalled at Falkland Junction for power stations and steel works in the Glasgow area, and recently with a service of merry-go-round trains to Longannet Power Station in Fife. Apart from the Waterside line, this coal comes in from the east by way of Annbank where one line runs to Mauchline, tapping traffic from the Auchinleck area, and another to Drongan which used to have a number of pits nearby but is now

dependant on the massive modern colliery at Killoch. Shortly after the closing of the 'Port Road' to Stranraer, the passenger traffic from the south to Stranraer ran via Mauchline and Annbank but during the past year this has been rerouted by Kilmarnock and Barassie Junction.

In mentioning Barassie, reference must also be made to the original line from the Kilmarnock area to Troon, one of the very earliest in Scotland and known as the 'Duke of Portland's Railway'. This was laid to 4ft 6in gauge and is reputed to have tried steam traction long before the better known Glasgow & Garnkirk line though this was not a success. When the Glasgow, Paisley, Kilmarnock and Ayr railway was formed to become the nucleus of the G&SW, the Duke of Portland's railway was relaid to standard gauge but still sticks very closely to the original formation. Finally, in considering Ayrshire & Galloway, mention must be made of Muirkirk, once a thriving iron smelting town in the hills, 24 miles east of Ayr. Even after the iron industry died there remained a flourishing mining complex which nearly made Muirkirk a major railway centre with, as usual, the Caley and the G&SW fighting for the spoils. The former even built a line over the hills from Strathaven which arrived just as Muirkirk's industrial decline set in and never ran a train! Till the early 1960s Muirkirk still had three rail outlets, the original Caley line to Lanark, a G&SW branch to Auchinleck and the A&C line more or less direct to Annbank. Now it has none. As a footnote, if Troon Harbour was the terminus of the first railway in Ayrshire with the end of steam it became the last stop. Many steam locomotives were towed from as far away as Carlisle to the West of Scotland ship-breaking yard for scrapping.

Above: The west end of Castle Douglas
station on 15 April 1963. Standard
Class 4MTT No 80023 leaves with an SLS
special to Kirkcudbright having taken over
from 5XP No 45588 *Kashmir* just visible in
the background that had worked the train
from Carlisle.

Top left: Dwarfed by the towering basalt Clints of Dromore, Class 5 No 44996 climbs from the Big Fleet viaduct towards Gatehouse of Fleet station (a mere 7 miles from the little town it served) with the morning Dumfries-Stranraer stopping train in May 1964.

Bottom left: The last summer of operation on the Port Road saw two Sundays of hectic activity when no less than three troop trains were run between Stranraer and Woodburn in Northumberland. On Sunday, 30 May 1965, one of these trains returning to Stranraer passes the Gatehouse of Fleet distant signal hauled by Clan No 72006 *Clan Mackenzie*.

Above: Until the closure of the line, the little station at Creetown was always immaculately kept with banks of flowers and well-tended relics of Victorian railways. In June 1964 Class 5 No 45463 eases the morning Stranraer-Dumfries stopping train into Creetown.

Above: If ever a branch line had a character all of its own it was the Whithorn branch from Newton Stewart to Whithorn. Built with delusions of grandeur, fought over by several major companies and loved by none, it survived as a local line for a long time and as late as 1964 had a thrice-weekly goods train. On 24 April 1963 this train returns to Newton Stewart near Wigtown behind Ivatt Mogul No 46467.

Above: The original idea of the Whithorn Branch was to get to Garlieston which was the first terminus of the line, the extension to Whithorn coming later. The attraction of Garlieston was its sheltered harbour which, like many of its kind in SW Scotland, gradually silted up over the years. About once a week till the end of the Whithorn line, the goods paid a visit down the overgrown line from Millisle to Garlieston. On 22 May 1964 Standard 2 Mogul No 78016 pushes through the trees near the derelict Garlieston station with what was nearly the last train to attempt this rustic ordeal.

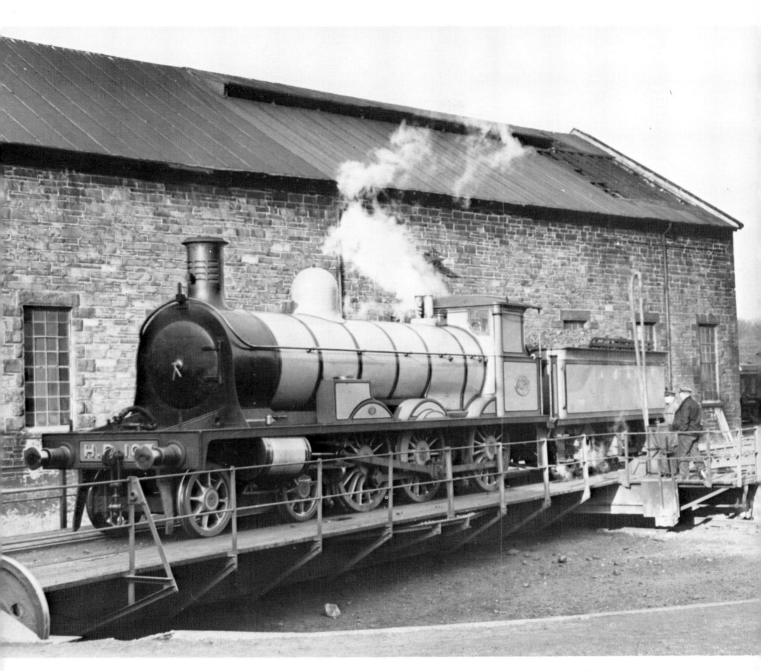

Top left: The SLS Special to Whithorn on 15 April 1963 pauses for water at Sorbie with Caley 2F No 57375 in charge. This train had the distinction of being probably the first and certainly the last to convey a buffet car down the Whithorn branch.

Bottom left: In June 1962 the SLS and RCTS ran a joint trip from Glasgow to Stranraer then down to Whithorn returning by way of Dumfries. The train is seen here crossing the Glenluce viaduct between Stranraer and Newton Stewart behind Caley Single No 123 and GNSR 4-4-0 No 49 *Gordon Highlander*.

Above: The Jones Goods 4-6-0 of the Highland Railway No 103 on the turntable at Stranraer shed on 13 April 1963 after working down from Glasgow light engine. Apart from the nose of the diesel shunter this could have been Inverness 70 years ago.

Top left: The Jones Goods and GNSR No 49 *Gordon Highlander* make a rousing start past Stranraer Harbour Junction with the SLS Special of 15 April 1963 returning to Glasgow after the tour of the Galloway branches.

Bottom left: Crossing at Glenwhilly. Nos 103 and 49 wait in the station to cross a dmu from Stranraer to Glasgow while working light engines to Stranraer on 13 April 1963.

Above: South-west Scotland on the whole has a mild if moist climate and little snow, the latter usually occurring late in the winter and with blizzard conditions. One such blizzard occurred in February 1963 completely cutting off Stranraer from the outside world. It took two days to get the line open across the moors south of Girvan and as Stranraer was running short of essential supplies one of the first trains through was a relief goods hauled by Class 5 No 45022 piloted by 5XP No 45588 *Kashmir*. The force of the wind had driven snow into every cutting and this photo shows the two engines struggling and slithering through the notorious 'Gunners Cut' a mile south of Barrhill.

Top left: The unusual side of the Pinmore viaduct that can only be taken on a winter's morning on account of vegetation. The 8am Stranraer-Falkland Junction (Ayr) goods crossing behind Class 5 No 45366 in February 1963.

Bottom left: The annual visit of the weed-killer to the Stranraer line on 20 May 1966 finds Class 5 No 45467 struggling up the hardest part of the 1 in 54 Glendoune Bank out of Girvan.

Above: The line into Girvan Goods station was distinguished by an unusual bridge over the River Girvan comprising plate girders on wooden trestle type supports. When this photo was taken in April 1966 these supports were in the process of being renewed. The train is a Branch Line Society tour of Ayrshire hauled by B1 No 61342.

Above: Class 5s Nos 44724 and 44727 launch an all-out attack on the 1 in 54 of the Glendoune Bank after taking water at Girvan with a Heysham-Stranraer fertiliser special in September 1965. They failed to make the top and had to divide the train at the waterworks, working it on to Pinwherry in two separate parts.

Above: Last journey for two of Stranraer's ex-
Caledonian 2F 0-6-0s on 9 September
1963. Hauled by Class 5 No 45384 they
drop down into Girvan en route to the West
of Scotland shipbreaking yard at Troon.

Top left: The morning Stranraer-Falkland Junction goods was often a heavy train that had to be double-headed. In April 1966 this train ascends the Killochan bank east of Girvan with Stephenson valve-geared Class 5 No 44767 piloting No 45162. No 44767 reputedly the best of the whole class is preserved and was in the Shildon Cavalcade in 1975 after being named *Stephenson.*

Bottom left: One of Ayr's most unpopular mineral trains was the afternoon coal train from Bargany Colliery in the Girvan Valley to Ayr Harbour, mainly on account of very complicated shunting operations at the mine and a very difficult start on a 1 in 60 grade up to Dailly. Standard 4 Mogul No 76096 and 'Crab' 42863 having shunted their load out of the colliery collect the van on the main line before tackling this climb.

Above: By April 1966 the output from Bargany mine had fallen considerably and double heading was rare. On an April afternoon 'Crab' No 42908 heads for Ayr Harbour through Dailly station at the top of the 1 in 60. (There is good reason to suppose that with mining subsidences over the years, the gradient is now somewhat steeper.)

Above: In March 1965 another blizzard struck the Stranraer line. It was of such severity that even after the cuttings had been ploughed out dmus normally forming the service were banned south of Ayr and steam trains ran instead. One of these, forming the 11.30am from Glasgow, stands in Maybole station behind Class 5 No 45486 still sporting the large wedge plough from clearing operations the day before.

Above: High summer at Dalrymple Junction in August 1958 as an immaculate Fairburn 2-6-4T passes the box with a Glasgow-Girvan local. At this time, shortly before the coming of the dmus on these services, Ayr shed kept its allocation of these tanks in beautiful condition for such duties.

Top left: Winter at Dalrymple Junction on 1 March 1965 'Crab' No 42917 approaches the junction from the west with a Girvan-Ayr goods comprised entirely of coal from Bargany.

Bottom left: 2P No 40590 crosses the Dalrymple viaduct with the evening Ayr-Dalmellington local train in 1958. This line has now been cut back to Waterside and is goods only, catering for a rapidly dwindling coal traffic.

Above: On another branch now closed, Ayr's prize B1 No 61261 heads the Saturdays-only Heads of Ayr-Edinburgh train near Greenan siding on 1 June 1965. Remarkably, through the summers of 1964/65 this engine was kept very smart for working extra passenger trains.

Above: A rare appearance of a 'Duchess' at Ayr. No 46223 *Princess Alice* crosses the river immediately east of the station with a Glasgow-Ayr Race special on Monday 15 July 1963.

Above: After the transfer to Fife of Ayr's B1s
the job of standby passenger engine fell to
Standard Mogul No 76096 which was kept
reasonably clean for such jobs as the Heads
of Ayr-Edinburgh summer Saturday train,
seen here leaving Ayr in July 1966.

Above: Ivatt Mogul No 46451 in Platform 5 at Ayr with a short parcels train from Kilmarnock in May 1966. Interestingly the loco still has Hurlford stencilled on the buffer beam despite the fact that the Kilmarnock shed had been closed for over two years.

Top right: As late as the summer of 1958, Caley 0-4-4T No 55262 was kept in immaculate condition as Ayr's station pilot. It is seen here propelling a rake of empty stock into platform No 1. With the coming of the dmus a year later the need for a station pilot ceased and 55262 was withdrawn for scrapping.

Bottom right: Another photo of the 8am Stranraer-Falkland Junction goods coasting through Ayr station in May 1966 behind Class 5s Nos 44999 and 45168.

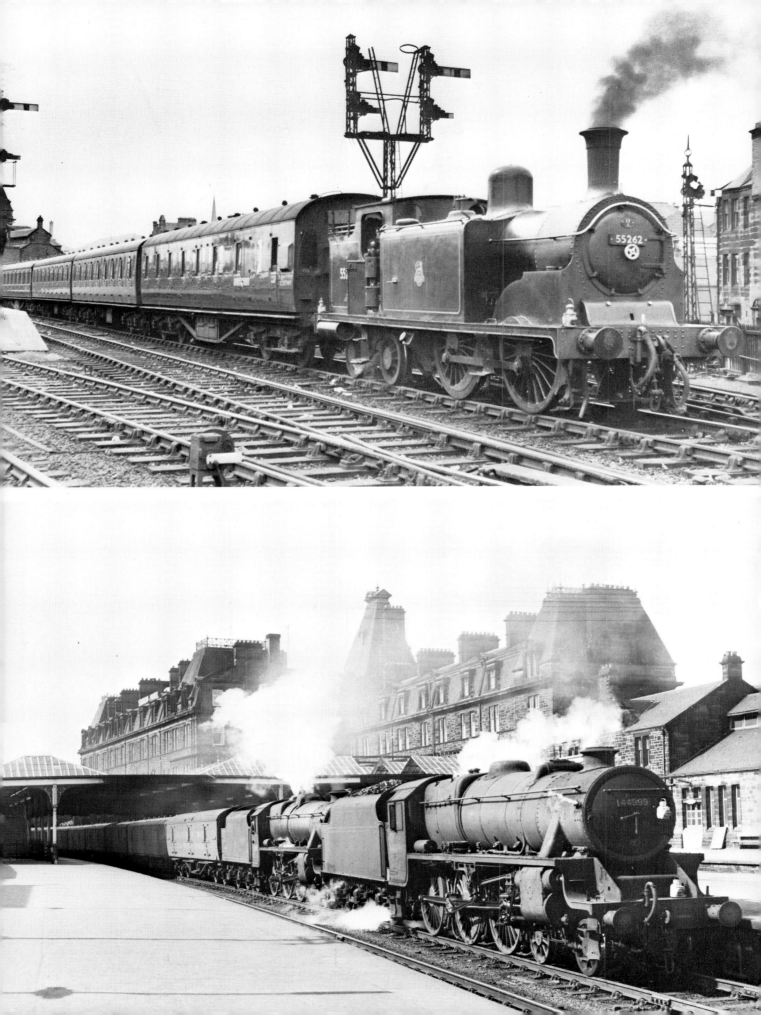

Above: Late autumn sunlight catches Class 5 No 45160 in Ayr shed in October 1964 with the tender of one of Ayr's numerous 'Crabs' visible in the left hand arch.

Top right: With the gradual rundown of the pits in South Ayrshire and the Girvan Valley, the main coal traffic tended to be concentrated in central Ayrshire. In June 1963 'Crab' No 42803 coasts past Mossblown Junction with a train from Killoch. The line in the background served Auchincruive colliery and was closed later that year resulting in the removal of the junction and signal box at Mossblown.

Bottom right: Near Mossblown in 1958, two Caley 0-6-0s Nos 57633 and 57569 drop down towards Ayr with the morning Littlemill-Falkland Junction coal train while an unidentified 'Crab' climbs towards Annbank with a rake of empties. This Littlemill train was known unofficially as 'the Twins' on account of its regular working by two Caley 3Fs.

Top left: 'Jubilee' No 45586 *Mysore* comes off the Mauchline line at Annbank Junction with an excursion from Halifax to Ayr in May 1963 while 'the Twins' from Littlemill colliery wait on the branch at Annbank station. Again this scene has changed out of recognition with the station demolished and even the coal tip in the background removed. Both lines remain but that to Mauchline is singled.

Bottom left: The Annbank smash of 21 March 1966. Standard Mogul No 76021 ran away on the steep descent from Tarbolton and collided side on with a goods train coming off the branch from Drongan hauled by a 'Crab', much to the delight of the pupils of the local school who had just finished for the day!

Above: The new modern pit at Killoch was badly sited both from a geological and railway point of view, the latter entailing a steep and curving climb from Drongan. On 16 April 1965 a test was carried out with a Standard Mogul No 76096 with 50 empties for Killoch seen leaving the loops at Drongan. It got to Killoch . . . just, and thereafter these jobs reverted to the 'Crabs'.

Top left: A very woebegone 'Crab' No 42919 takes water at Belston Junction on a bitter January day in 1966 with a coal train from Littlemill to Ayr. Note the smoke from the brazier under the water tower to keep supplies from freezing.

Bottom left: 'The Twins' at Belston Junction with 3Fs Nos 57569 and 57633 in 1961. These workings from Littlemill were interesting as they propelled their loads the two miles from the pit to Belston Junction before reversing direction and heading for Annbank and Ayr over the old A&C line seen at the base of the box.

Above: At the height of the coal boom in Ayrshire several lines were built mainly to tap this traffic though some carried a passenger service. One such was the A&C line that ran from Annbank to Cronberry Junction (Nr Muirkirk) and at one time boasted a regular through train from Ayr to Edinburgh. Passenger traffic ceased after the war and with the closure of the mines it served, the A&C was closed completely at the end of 1962. In April 1964 Standard 3 Mogul No 77007 eases empty wagons down the line for its demolition near Lugar.

Above: Great things were expected of Muirkirk in the way of iron and coal mining and several railways were built there, none of which survive today and Muirkirk itself is a ghost town. In 1961, however, it still had a passenger service to Lanark and on a March morning Standard 3 Mogul No 77015 waits with the 9.05am train to Lanark and Carstairs in Muirkirk station.

Top right: The most scenic feature of the line from Muirkirk to Lanark was the crossing of Glenbuck Loch. No 77015 in the middle of the loch with a midday train from Lanark to Muirkirk in 1961.

Bottom right: Very shortly before the passenger services were withdrawn in 1962, two of the Stanier 3PT 2-6-2Ts appeared in the district, one of which makes a very smoky start out of Inches with a Lanark-bound train. The line in the background serves Kennox colliery which kept a daily goods train running after the passenger service was withdrawn. In 1965 the pit closed and the whole Muirkirk-Lanark section was lifted.

Above: The end, not just of a chapter or of a book but of the steam era and a magnificent locomotive. 'Duchess' No 46226 *Duchess of Norfolk*, minus nameplates, motion and about everything else movable approaching the West of Scotland shipbreaking yard at Troon having been towed from Kingmoor by Standard 5 No 73143 which according to the driver was in a b..... sight worse mechanical condition than the 'Duchess'.